SIXTH EDITION

STUDY GUIDE TO ACCOMPANY

THE LEGAL ENVIRONMENT OF BUSINESS

Roger E. Meiners
University of Texas at Arlington

Al H. Ringleb
Clemson University

Frances L. Edwards
Clemson University

PREPARED BY

Lynda S. Hamilton
Georgia Southern University

West Publishing Company

Minneapolis/St. Paul   New York   Los Angeles   San Francisco

WEST'S COMMITMENT TO THE ENVIRONMENT

In 1906, West Publishing Company began recycling materials left over from the production of books. This began a tradition of efficient and responsible use of resources. Today, 100% of our legal bound volumes are printed on acid-free, recycled paper consisting of 50% new fibers. West recycles nearly 27,700,000 pounds of scrap paper annually—the equivalent of 229,300 trees. Since the 1960s, West has devised ways to capture and recycle waste inks, solvents, oils, and vapors created in the printing process. We also recycle plastics of all kinds, wood, glass, corrugated cardboard, and batteries, and have eliminated the use of polystyrene book packaging. We at West are proud of the longevity and the scope of our commitment to the environment.

West pocket parts and advance sheets are printed on recyclable paper and can be collected and recycled with newspapers. Staples do not have to be removed. Bound volumes can be recycled after removing the cover.

Production, Prepress, Printing and Binding by West Publishing Company.

 TEXT IS PRINTED ON 10% POST CONSUMER RECYCLED PAPER

COPYRIGHT © 1997 by WEST PUBLISHING CO.
                         610 Opperman Drive
                         P.O. Box 64526
                         St. Paul, MN 55164–0526

ISBN 0–314–20770–8

TABLE OF CONTENTS

CH. 1 - The Modern Environment of Business

OVERVIEW AND CHAPTER OUTLINE

This chapter provides an overview of the general nature of law and the legal system. Next, the chapter discusses the fundamental objectives of law, the creation of law, the functions of law in an orderly society, the classifications of law, and the major sources of law. We consider the influence of the needs and demands of businesses, consumers and the government, and some of the major ethical issues in the business environment.

I. **LAW AND THE KEY FUNCTIONS OF THE LEGAL SYSTEM**

    A.   Assuring Social Control by Influencing Behavior

    B.   Conflict Resolution

    C.   Social Maintenance

    D.   Social Change

    E.   International Perspectives: Chad: A Third World Country Looks to Create a Legal System

II. **SOURCES OF LAW IN THE UNITED STATES**

    A.   Common Law

KEY WORDS AND PHRASES

Black's Law Dictionary
Formal rules
Informal (implicit) rules
Private disputes
Public disputes
Judge-made or common law
Curia Regis
English common law
Precedent
Stare decisis
Constitution
Separation of powers
Statutory law
Executive orders
Religious law

Civil law
Public law
Private law
Criminal law
Beyond a reasonable doubt
Felony
Misdemeanor
Substantive law
Procedural law
Corporate responsibility
Narrow (agents-of-capital) view
Social contract
Invisible hand
Public interest
Corporate culture

FILL-INS

1. _____ The original source of law in this country that is made and applied by judges as they resolve disputes between private parties and is referred to as judge-made law.

2. _____ Courts developed by William the Conqueror and his successors to unify England. They were to develop and then apply a common or uniform set of rules for the entire country.

3. _____ Is the fundamental law of the nation and establishes the limits of governmental power.

4. _____ A prior decided case that is similar in its facts to a case presently under consideration.

5. _____ Congress used its constitutionally granted powers to create these, which are often called the fourth branch of government.

6. _____ The President can create law by issuing one of these.

7. _____ This body of law governs legal wrongs, or crimes, committed against all of society.

8._____   This doctrine refers to the use of precedent in deciding present cases and literally means "to stand on decided cases."

10._____   This new African country is trying to create a legal system.

11. _____   He urges that the social responsibility of a business executive (and hence a corporation) is "to make as much money as possible while conforming to the basic rules of society, both those embodied in law and those embodied in ethical custom."

12. _____   Refers to generally accepted standards of right and wrong in society.

13. _____   He said: "I can urge [people] to disobey segregation ordinances, for the [ordinances] are morally wrong."

14. _____   He says that corporations are not moral agents that can be held morally accountable for their actions.

15. _____   He maintains that there has always been a kind of "social contract" between business and society.

16._____   This refers to general and abstract concepts that might be encountered in codes of ethics in business and professions.

17._____   He provides support for the view that it makes sense to attribute moral responsibilities to corporations.

18._____   This "contract" represents an implicit understanding of the proper goals and responsibilities of business.

19._____   According to his classic argument, corporations can contribute more to the public good if left to do what they do best, namely make a profit within the bounds of the law and the most basic moral guidelines prohibiting fraud and deception.

20._____   This refers to the values and attitudes that pervade the corporate workplace.

MULTIPLE CHOICE QUESTIONS

Select the best answer to each of the following questions.

1. _____   The term <u>law</u> can be defined as:

       a.   A body of rules of conduct prescribed by controlling authority, and having binding legal force.

       b.   A statement of circumstances, in which the public force is brought to bear through the courts.

       c.   A rule of conduct that will be enforced by the courts if its authority is challenged.

       d.   A and C only

       e.   All of the above are correct.

2. _____   Which of the following is <u>not</u> a source of law?

       a.   Constitutions.

       b.   Statutory law.

       c.   Administrative agency regulations.

       d.   Stare decisis.

       e.   Common law.

3. _____   Suppose a dispute arises between a company that pollutes the air and a nearby farmer who is adversely affected by the pollution. If no federal or state statute controls this kind of pollution, the dispute involves:

       a.   Private law and civil law.

       b.   Public law and criminal law.

       c.   Procedural law and criminal law.

       d.   Common law, precedent, and public law.

       e.   Public law only.

4._____   Which of the following is an example of substantive law?

    a.   Administrative law.

    b.   Civil procedure.

    c.   Criminal procedure.

    d.   Administrative procedure.

5._____   Prior judicial decisions are binding authority in subsequent cases under the principle of:

    a.   Ethical custom.

    b.   Social control by influencing behavior.

    c.   Stare decisis.

    d.   Judicial review.

    e.   Curia Regis.

6. _____   Which of the following in not an argument of Dr. Milton Friedman?

    a.   The social responsibility of a business executive is to make as much money as possible while conforming to basic rules of society.

    b.   Business has an obligation not to undertake actions that might be grossly offensive to the general public.

    c.   A business executive is an agent of his principal, the shareholders.

    d.   There has always been a kind of "social contract" between business and society.

7. _____   Kenneth Goodpaster isolates four elements of moral responsibility. Which of the following is <u>not</u> one of them?

    a.   Ethics.

    b.   Moral reasoning.

    c.   Perception.

    d.   Coordination.

8. _____   The following term is taken to refer to generally accepted standards of right and wrong in society:

    a.   Morals.

    b.   Ethics.

    c.   Etiquette.

    d.   Rules of law.

9. _____   The U. S. Supreme Court in <u>Stanley</u> held that:

    a.   It is not immoral or illegal for the Army to test LSD on unsuspecting soldiers.

    b.   Testing human subjects without their consent is unconstitutional.

    c.   Sgt. Stanley can sue the officers personally but not the Army.

    d.   The U. S. Military is legally immune from any suit by an injured soldier under the Federal Tort Claims Act.

10. _____   Which of the following is <u>not</u> a part of Dr. John Ladd's teaching?

    a.   Corporations are not moral agents that can be held morally accountable for their actions.

    b.   An organization is rational when it acts in accord with moral ideals.

    c.   Corporations can act only in accordance with a means-ends formula.

    d.   Businesses can act only in accord with specified organizational goals: survival, autonomy, and growth.

===

MATCHING

Match the following terms or phrases to the descriptions below.

a.   Constitution

b.   Benjamin Nathan Cardozo

c.   Informal rules of society

d.   Legal environment of business

e.   Criminal law

f.   Civil law approach

g.   Executive order

h.   Substantive law

i.   <u>Black's Law Dictionary</u>

j.   Oliver Wendell Holmes

k.   Corporate culture

l.   <u>Soldano v. O'Daniels</u>

m.   Davis-Bacon Act

n.   Professor William Frederick

o.   Nuremburg Military Trial

p.   Perception

q.   Implementation

r.   Grimshaw v. Ford Motor Company

s.   Kenneth Goodpaster

t.   Coordination

1._____   One of the most important sources of law affecting it are regulations, agency opinions, and agency orders flowing from the administrative agencies.

2._____   Classification of law that includes common law and statutory law that define and establish legal rights and regulate behavior.

3._____   The president can create law by issuing one of these.

4._____   Concerns legal wrongs committed against all of society.

5._____   Rules dictated by a society's history, values, customs, traditions, commercial aspirations, and ethics; involves characteristics of trust, honesty, and integrity.

6._____   He defines law as a statement of the circumstances, in which the public force is brought to bear through the courts.

7._____   He defined law as a principle or rule of conduct so established as to justify a prediction with reasonable certainty that it will be enforced by the courts if its authority is challenged.

8._____   The fundamental law of a nation that established both the powers of the government and the limits of that power.

9._____   Defines law, in its generic sense, as a body of rules of action or conduct prescribed by controlling authority, and having binding legal force.

10._____   The Japanese legal system follows an approach modeled on German law.

11. _____   He states that it makes sense to attribute moral responsibility to corporations.

12. _____   It held that the question of whether a bartender had a duty to allow a phone call to be made when another's life was being threatened should be resolved by a jury.

13. _____   Corporations exhibit this characteristic when they gather information before making a decision.

14. _____   It upheld a large award of punitive damages after serious injuries occurred when a car's gas tank exploded.

15. _____   It refers to the values and attitudes that pervade the corporate workplace.

16. _____   This requires that a moral agent be able to carry out a strategic decision in the "real world" by understanding the environment, implementing the strategy, and by guiding it towards realization.

17. _____   This Act requires all federal building contractors to pay "prevailing wages."

18. _____   Under them, German war criminals were found guilty of experimenting with unknowing human subjects.

19. _____   He found that corporations with codes of ethics were cited for legal infractions more frequently than those with out codes.

20. _____   This requires a moral agent to be able to integrate the moral evaluation with various nonmoral considerations, such as self-interest, the law, economics, and politics.

CASE PROBLEMS

1.   Is it a fair assessment of our modern business environment to say that law functions well in resolving conflicts and assuring social control, but it is not an acceptable mechanism to bring about social change?

_____

_____

_____

2. Because judges use precedent and follow the theory of stare decisis in deciding cases, is there room for their own opinions and prejudices to influence the outcome of cases?

     _____

     _____

     _____

3. When law is used to influence business conduct, the regulations may control safety in the work place, environmental pollution and employment relations. May the law ever control prices, given that the U. S. is a free market economy?

     _____

     _____

     _____

4. Was Justice Cardozo correct when he said that law allowed us to predict with reasonable certainty whether or not courts would enforce the rules of conduct if their authority was challenged?

     _____

     _____

     _____

5. Carl was injured while working for Harry's Diner. He applied for Workers' Compensation for his medical expenses and lost time. To his dismay, he found that Harry did not carry Workers' Compensation insurance. Harry claimed that he did not know he was supposed to carry it; he had only been in business for a few months, and no one had told him to purchase it. Does Harry have a legal and moral obligation to Carl?

     _____

     _____

     _____

APPLICATION QUESTIONS

DO YOU AGREE OR DISAGREE WITH THE FOLLOWING STATEMENTS? JOT DOWN YOUR REASONS.

1. In the <u>Soldano</u> case, the judge overturned old, established precedents for the sake of his own moral opinions about the behavior of the bartender.

   Agree_____   Disagree_____

   Reasons:

2. It is a moral principle to state that euthanasia is wrong, and a moral judgment to say that "Doctor Death's" assistance of the suicide of a terminally ill patient is wrong.

   Agree_____   Disagree_____

   Reasons:

3. Under the Anshen view of a "social contract" between a corporation and its surrounding community, management has an obligation to consider the rights of workers, customers, and residents of the surrounding community as well as those of the stockholders. This means that a pharmaceutical company would not be morally justified in closing its plant in Connecticut and moving its operation to Puerto Rico.

   Agree_____   Disagree_____

   Reasons:

4.   It is a moral principle that destruction of the environment is not good. Some would argue correctly that it is a morally responsible judgment to develop a trade-off between the protection of endangered species and the protection of jobs.

Agree_____   Disagree_____

Reasons:

5.   Under the Friedman view of corporate social responsibility, Exxon's decision not to double hull its oil supertankers need be morally justified by no other motive than the economic benefit of the stockholders.

Agree_____   Disagree_____

Reasons:

CH. 2 - The Court System

OVERVIEW AND CHAPTER OUTLINE

This chapter provides an overview of the American court systems and discusses how an injured party can gain access to the relief the systems can provide.

I. **THE LITIGATION PROCESS**

    A. Rules of Civil Procedure

II. **THE CONCEPT OF JURISDICTION**

III. **SUBJECT-MATTER JURISDICTION**

    A. Organization of the Court System

    B. Subject-Matter Jurisdiction of the State Court Systems

        1. State Courts of Original Jurisdiction

            a. Juris*prudence*? Thanks for the Help, Judge

            b. State Courts of Appellate Jurisdiction

IX.   SUMMARY

X.   ISSUE: HOW DOES THE SUPREME COURT SELECT CASES FOR REVIEW?

KEY WORDS AND PHRASES

Civil litigation
Plaintiff
Defendant
Federal Rules of Civil Procedure
Jurisdiction
Subject matter jurisdiction
Original jurisdiction
Appellate jurisdiction
General jurisdiction
Limited or special jurisdiction
Trial de novo
Small claims courts
Federal question
Diversity-of-citizenship
Amount in controversy
Right to appeal
Original and exclusive jurisdiction
Writ of certiorari
Cour de cessation
Cour d'appel
Tribunal d'instance
In personam jurisdiction
Summons
Service of process
Default judgment
Personal service

Substituted service
Long-arm statute
Minimum contacts
In rem jurisdiction
Quasi in rem
Constructive notice
Exclusive jurisdiction
Concurrent jurisdiction
Removal
Real and substantial party
Conflict-of law rules
Restatement (Second) of Conflict of Laws
Venue
Forum non conveniens
Missouri System
Doctrine of judicial immunity
Equitable remedies
Monetary damages
Compensatory damages
Punitive or exemplary damages
Nominal damages
Expectancy damages
Curia Regis
Equity
Specific performance
Injunction

FILL-INS

1._____   Rules which were developed by the U.S. Supreme Court, became effective in 1938, and have been adopted by most of the states.

2._____   A state statutory requirement that, on the basis of fairness, lawsuits must be brought in a court in the county in which either the plaintiff or the defendant resides.

3._____   Jurisdiction exercised when a defendant's property within a state is attached to secure payment for an unrelated matter.

4. _____   How service of process is traditionally achieved.

5. _____   A state law that permits its courts to reach beyond a state's boundaries and obtain jurisdiction over nonresident defendants.

6. _____   May enact legislation specifically intended to change the appellate jurisdiction of the U.S. Supreme Court.

7. _____   Appellate review by the U.S. Supreme Court is normally obtained by this petition.

8._____   A court of special jurisdiction which hears appeals from district courts in patent, trademark and copyright cases.

9. _____   The power to speak the law.

10._____   A constitutional or statutory limitation on the type of disputes a court can resolve.

11._____   Power over a particular subject matter is, by statute, given to a specific court system to the exclusion of others.

12. _____   Courts where disputes are initially brought and tried.

13._____   Federal courts that review decisions at the intermediate appellate court level.

14._____   State courts with very limited jurisdiction as to both subject matter and nature of the amount in controversy.

15._____   A new trial granted to the losing party in a court proceeding.

16._____   The only courts in the federal system to use juries.

17._____   A doctrine developed to provide a neutral forum for handling disputes between citizens of different states.

18._____ The right of both federal and state courts to hear a case.

19._____ This law created the federal court system.

20._____ A judgment for the plaintiff when the defendant fails to appear in court.

MULTIPLE CHOICE QUESTIONS

Select the best answer to each of the following questions.

1. _____ Federal question jurisdiction involves:

   a. cases arising under Constitutional law.

   b. cases between citizens of different states.

   c. only federal jury trials.

   d. questionable factual determinations made by the trial jury in a lower court.

   e. any evidence the attorneys for either side wish to present.

2. _____ Which of the following is not a principal function of the civil litigation process?

   a. To bring a peaceful resolution to disputes between society members.

   b. To uphold the dignity of the law and the legal system.

   c. To provide a mechanism for enforcing court decisions.

   d. To develop new laws for society.

3. _____   Exclusive jurisdiction is:

    a.   The power to lawfully bind a party to a dispute.

    b.   The power over a particular subject matter that is provided by statute to a specific court system to the exclusion of others.

    c.   The power to hear all controversies that may be brought before a court.

    d   A court's power over the person of a defendant.

    e.   None of the above.

4. _____   Small claims courts are:

    a.   Particularly advantageous for small debts.

    b.   A much more expedient forum than the district courts with disputes generally being heard within two months after the filing date.

    c.   Courts having very limited jurisdiction, with restrictions imposed on both the subject matter they can hear and the amount-in-controversy.

    d.   All of the above.

5. _____   Which of the following is not true about the U.S. Supreme Court?

    a.   It is the highest court in both the federal and state court systems.

    b.   It is primarily an appellate review court.

    c.   Cases before it are generally heard by nine justices.

    d.   It has complete discretion to hear only those cases it selects for review.

6. _____   Monetary remedies available in civil litigation include:

        a.   injunctions.

        b.   expectancy damages.

        c.   specific performance.

        d.   equity.

        e.   none of the above is correct.

7. _____   When both state and federal courts have the power to hear a case, their jurisdiction is:

        a.   Jurisdiction over the person.

        b.   Exclusive.

        c.   Removal.

        d.   Concurrent.

8. _____   Where there is concurrent jurisdiction, the right of a defendant sued in a state court to choose to litigate in federal court is called:

        a.   A conflict-of-law problem.

        b.   Exclusive jurisdiction.

        c.   Removal jurisdiction.

        d.   Appellate jurisdiction.

9. _____   Restatement Second Conflict of Law rules:

        a.   Include choice of law questions.

        b.   Depend on diversity of all parties.

        c.   Waive reasonable predictability in the interest of fairness.

        d.   All of the above.

10. _____   Which of the following is <u>not</u> one of the situations in which a court can exercise jurisdiction over a corporation:

    a.   The court is located in the state in which the corporation was incorporated.

    b.   The court is located in the state where the corporation has its headquarters or its main plant.

    c.   The court is located in a state where the defendant has less than minimum contacts.

    d.   The court is located in a state in which the corporation has been doing business.

11. _____   London's Commercial Court:

    a.   Is frequently chosen as a forum for dispute resolution.

    b.   Provides one judge for each trial.

    c.   Does not allow jury trials.

    d.   Requires the losing party to pay the winner's attorney fees.

    e.   All of the above.

12. _____   In <u>Rose v. Giamatti</u>, the court held that:

    a.   Pete Rose wagered on major baseball games.

    b.   complete diversity of citizenship is <u>not</u> necessary to remove a case from state to federal court.

    c.   a proper defendant must be a "real party in interest".

    d.   all of the above.

    e.   b and c only.

MATCHING

Match the following terms or phrases to the descriptions below.

a. Court of Appeals for the Federal Circuit

b. U.S. Supreme Court

c. In personam jurisdiction

d. Judicial immunity

e. International Shoe Co. v. Washington

f. Property subject to an in rem proceeding

g. Shaffer v. Heitner

h. Federal judges

i. Equitable remedies

j. Cour de cessation

k. Removal jurisdiction

l. Conflict of law problem

m. Erie v. Thompkins

n. Beatty v. College Center

o. Judges

p. Congress

q. Right to appeal

r. Oregon v. Lillard

s. Rose v. Giamatti.

t. Nondiscretionary review

u.   Punitive damages

v.   Chancery court

1. _____   In some instances, because of the court that rendered the decision, the holding, or the parties involved, the Supreme Court is obligated to consider a case.

2. _____   A court's power over the person of a defendant that is usually established by serving the defendant with a summons.

3. _____   The doctrine that protects judges from being sued for judicial acts.

4. _____   This case held that a state's long arm statute must identify certain "minimum contacts" between the corporation and the state where the suit is being filed to qualify as due process.

5. _____   A court having nationwide territorial jurisdiction but limited subject matter jurisdiction. It hears cases on appeal from the U.S. District Courts in patent, trademark, and copyright cases, and those in which the U.S. is a defendant.

6. _____   Is primarily an appellate review court and cases reaching it are generally heard by nine justices.

7. _____   Tangible and intangible property.

8. _____   This case held that where a party sues on the basis of quasi in rem jurisdiction, a "minimum contacts" standard must be met.

9. _____   A supreme court of limited powers under the civil law of France.

10. _____   Where there is concurrent jurisdiction, a defendant sued in a state court has the right to choose to litigate in the federal system.

11. _____   A situation that may arise when a dispute is brought in a state court involving incidents which have taken place in more than one state or entirely in a different state, involving two or more bodies of law.

12. _____   This case held that, except in matters governed by the federal Constitution or by acts of Congress, the law to be applied is both the state's common and statutory law when deciding diversity of citizenship cases.

13._____   This case held that Restatement Second of Conflict of Laws criteria may be determinative in deciding which state has the most "significant relations" to the case.

14._____   Specific performance and injunction.

15._____   These individuals have the responsibility of applying and interpreting the rules that govern the legal proceedings over which they preside.

16._____   These individuals are nominated by the president and confirmed by a majority vote in the U.S. Senate.

17._____   This body may change the structure of the federal court system but may not reduce a judge's salary or term of office once an appointment has been made.

18._____   In this case the court held that "purposefully directed activities" in the plaintiff's state were "minimum contacts" for purposes of long arm jurisdiction.

19._____   This case held that the defendants in a lawsuit must be "real parties in interest."

20._____   Parties to a lower court's decision have this when a higher court is obligated to review their case if either party elects to appeal.

21._____   Medieval English courts that dealt with questions of justice where money would not provide adequate relief.

22. _____   Monetary damages imposed on businesses to punish reprehensible or malicious conduct and to deter similar future conduct.

CASE PROBLEMS

1.   The National Inquirer printed a story about Carol Burnett in which it asserted that she had been drunk and disorderly in an expensive Washington, D.C. restaurant and that Henry Kissinger was involved in an altercation with her. The story was totally false. She suffered no physical injuries as a result of being libeled, but she sued the National Inquirer. What kind of monetary or equitable damages should she be able to recover?

_____

_____

_____

2. Michelle Marvin sued Lee Marvin in a California state court claiming that she and Marvin entered into a contract providing that she would give up her singing career and make a home for him, and he would support her for the rest of her life. Lee Marvin terminated their relationship and refused to continue to support her. What kind of damages should she be entitled to? Can Lee get the case to federal court?

_____

_____

_____

3. Smith, a citizen of Texas is injured in a car accident in Tulsa, Oklahoma, in a car driven by Jones, a citizen of Missouri. In which court or courts may Smith sue? Which state's law would apply?

_____

_____

_____

4. Johnson and Jackson were adjoining landowners. Johnson sued Jackson, alleging that trees on Jackson's land were overhanging Johnson's property and interfering with his use of his property. Jackson lived out of state, and he had not been within the state in years. Because Johnson did not know where Jackson lived, Johnson mailed a copy of the summons to a bank at which he thought Jackson once had an account. When Jackson did not show up at trial, a default judgment was entered for Johnson. Was this judgment valid?

_____

_____

_____

5.   Rath Corp. breached a contract to manufacture and deliver certain products to Lyons, a resident of California. Lyons sued Rath Corp. in a trial court of the state of California, a court of general jurisdiction. Under what circumstances will the California court have jurisdiction?

_____

_____

_____

6.   Carl, a citizen of North Carolina, is injured in Georgia by Adam, a citizen of Alabama. Carl's insurance carrier was in New York, and Adam's carrier was in Alabama. If Carl could sue Adam the Smasher in Georgia, and win under Georgia law, his claim for monetary damages would be greater than if he sues in Alabama. Given a conflict of law problem, what are the basic arguments?

_____

_____

_____

APPLICATION QUESTIONS

DO YOU AGREE OR DISAGREE WITH THE FOLLOWING STATEMENTS? JOT DOWN YOUR REASONS

1.   Courts must have jurisdiction over the subject matter of a law suit, over both parties to the suit, and in some cases, over the property owned by the defendant.

Agree _____   Disagree _____

Reasons:

2.   Reddy Roofer, Inc. roofed the food service building of the Duck Inn, but the roof leaked after a few months. Duck Inn is a Georgia Corporation. Reddy Roofer is a South Carolina corporation. Duck Inn wants to force Reddy into the Georgia court to answer for the harm done. When long-arm jurisdiction is utilized over out-of-state corporate defendants, the plaintiff must show that the defendant has been "doing business" within the forum state, so that it's managers could reasonably anticipate being "haled into court there." Can Duck do this?

Yes_____   No_____

Reasons:

3.   Solomon Shoesalesman went into Idaho to sell shoes to the Queen of Sheeba Shoe Store. Queenie signed the contract there for forty pairs of dancing shoes, and Sol went back to Missouri to his company's home office to have the contract signed by his manager, then sent the purchase order to Mexico to the factory where the shoes were made. The shoes were sent from the factory. When they arrived in Idaho, they were damaged and Queenie could not use them. Can she exercise long-arm jurisdiction over Sol in Idaho?

Yes_____   No_____

Reasons:

4.   The Court of Appeals for the Federal Circuit has limited subject matter jurisdiction but unlimited geographic jurisdiction in all cities where any of the twelve U. S. Circuit Courts of Appeal may sit.

Agree _____   Disagree _____

Reasons:

5.   Suppose Cheatam Land Co. contracts to buy a parcel of land from Farmer Brown, who later changes his mind and refuses to sell. The appropriate action is specific performance.

Agree _____   Disagree _____

Reasons:

CH. 3 - The Trial Process

OVERVIEW AND CHAPTER OUTLINE

This chapter begins by discussing the adversarial nature of our judicial system. It then examines the important stages of the litigation process, from pleadings, through the discovery, trial and appellate stages.

I.   **THE NATURE OF OUR ADVERSARY SYSTEM**

    A.   Does the Law Furnish Relief for the Disagreement?

    B.   What is the Probability of Winning the Lawsuit?

    C.   Would the Relief Provided Make the Lawsuit Worthwhile?

II.   **BUSINESS AS A DEFENDANT**

    A.   How Will Litigation Affect the Company's Goodwill?

    B.   How Important Is the Business Relationship?

    C.   Is Settlement a Viable Alternative?

    D.   Are We Encouraging Spurious Lawsuits?

    E.   Is the Lawsuit a Part of a Strategic Plan?

III.   **RESOLVING DISPUTES THROUGH THE COURTS**

    A.   Differences Between Business and Nonbusiness

        1.   Complexity of Litigation

        2.   Greater Use of Documents and Exhibits as Evidence

        3.   Heavier Reliance on Expert Testimony

        4.   Longer Trials

        5.   Larger Damage Awards

            a.   Juris*prudence*? Me, Biased?

    B.   The Growing Significance of Business Litigation

IV.   **BASIC TRIAL PROCEDURES**

    A.   Pleadings Stage

    B.   Responses to the Complaint

        1.   Motion to Dismiss

        2.   Answer

        3.   Affirmative Defenses

        4.   Counterclaim

            a.   Juris*prudence*? I said, No, No, No, It Ain't Me Babe!

        5.   Reply

        6.   Motion for Judgment on the Pleading

    C.   Discovery Stage: Obtaining Information Before Trial

        1.   Purpose of Discovery

        2.   Tools of the Discovery Process

KEY WORDS AND PHRASES

Adversary system of justice
Finder of fact
Jury
Judge
Defense
Settle
Service of process
Complaint
Motion to dismiss
Motion to dismiss for failure
    to state a claim or cause of action
Demurrer
Answer
Affirmative defense
Reply
Pleadings
Motion for judgment on the pleadings
Discovery
Counterclaim
Deposition

Written interrogatories
Protective order
Contempt of court
Pretrial conference
Summary judgment
Jury
Voir dire
Challenge for cause
Opening Statements
Direct examination
Cross-examination
Re-direct examination
Re-cross examination
Rest
Directed verdict
Closing argument
Jury instructions (or charges)
Burden of persuasion
Bailiff
Preponderance of the evidence

Hung	Judgment
Mistrial	Res judicata
Post-trial motions	Writ of execution
Judgment not withstanding the verdict	Oral arguments
(or judgment N.O.V)	Affirm
Error of law	Reverse
Written briefs	Modify
Dissenting opinions	Majority opinion
Remand	Concurring opinions

===

FILL-INS

1. _____ Statements by attorneys telling a jury what the crucial facts to the dispute are and how they will prove that these facts support their contentions and allegations.

2. _____ To reach this conclusion, the judge instructs the jury on the law, and the jury applies the law to the facts as it determines them to be.

3. _____ A written statement setting forth the plaintiff's claim against the defendant.

4. _____ This occurs when, after deliberating, a jury is unable to reach a unanimous decision.

5. _____ An allegation on the part of the defendant that even if the facts were true, the injury claimed by the plaintiff is an injury for which the law does not furnish a remedy.

6. _____ The Federal Rules of Civil Procedure use this test to deny requests for discovery.

7. _____ Questions in writing submitted by one party to the other.

8. _____ The pleading in which the defendant must admit or deny the allegations made by the plaintiff in the complaint.

9. _____ The standard of proof for a jury verdict in a civil trial.

10._____   This legal system requires each of the opposing parties to contest the position of the other before a court in a true case or controversy.

11._____   In essence, it is a response to a complaint by the defendant which then requires the plaintiff to respond just as the defendant did to the original complaint.

12._____   This requires a party to produce documents.

13._____   This is a determination by the court that no question of fact exists to be tried by a jury.

14._____   This occurs when the defendant admits injuring the plaintiff but that the additional facts he or she asserts constitute a defense to plaintiff's complaint.

15._____   Commands an official such as the sheriff to seize the property of the defendant and, if necessary, to sell the property to satisfy the judgment.

16._____   A process used to select members of a jury.

17._____   Involves a meeting with the attorneys and the judge and is intended to be a forum for simplifying the issues making up the dispute and to plan the course of the trial.

18._____   If a witness is unavailable at the time of the trial, this may, in some circumstances, be used in place of live testimony.

19._____   These may involve admission of evidence, jury instructions, and motions to dismiss as grounds for appeal.

20._____   Attorneys try to organize the evidence that has to be presented to the jury in a concise manner, thereby fashioning an argument most favorable to their case.

MULTIPLE CHOICE QUESTIONS

Select the best answer to each of the following questions.

1. _____   When a business is a defendant, it may choose to fight the suit or settle based on which of the following issues?

     a.   Estimated costs of defense.

     b.   Estimated chance of winning.

     c.   Effect of litigation on goodwill

     d.   Effect of litigation on customer relations.

     e.   All of the above.

2. _____   Opening statements:

     a.   Are evidence in the case.

     b.   Usually are given by the plaintiff's attorney and then followed by the opening statement of the defendant's attorney.

     c.   Are given by the plaintiff to the judge to establish the essential reasons why the trial is necessary.

     d.   Are the judge's introductory remarks to the parties, the attorneys, and the jury.

3. _____   Discovery:

     a.   Usually begins as soon as the jury is sworn in.

     b.   Is only available in criminal cases.

     c.   Provides an opportunity to preserve and determine relevant evidence.

     d.   Is permitted of the jury as they deliberate their verdict after permission is granted by the judge.

4. _____   Pretrial motions may include:

    a.   A motion to dismiss for failure to state a claim.

    b.   A motion for a judgment notwithstanding the verdict.

    c.   A motion for summary judgment.

    d.   A and C.

5. _____   What may the trial judge <u>not</u> do if he or she is dissatisfied with a jury's verdict?

    a.   Grant a motion for a new trial.

    b.   Grant a motion for a judgment notwithstanding the verdict.

    c.   Require a plaintiff who has received an excessive damage award to take a lesser sum.

    d.   Prohibit an appeal.

    e.   The judge of the trial court can do all of the above.

6. _____   When corporate executives are the subject of discovery, they may legally refuse to submit to personal interrogatories if:

    a.   They hire good lawyers.

    b.   The information requested can be supplied by lower level managers who have personal knowledge.

    c.   The plaintiff is not severely injured.

    d.   A and C.

    e.   All of the above.

7. _____   A civil case begins with:

    a.   A complaint, summons and reply.

    b.   A summons, answer and counterclaim.

    c.   A complaint, answer and order to produce.

    d.   A complaint, summons, and service of process on the defendant.

8. _____   Res judicata:

    a.   Means that once an issue had been decided by a court, it can't be relitigated.

    b.   Is another name for hearsay.

    c.   Means that evidence must be admissible to be considered by the jury.

    d.   Has little importance today, being an early English common law doctrine that became outdated during the Industrial Revolution.

9. _____   In giving jury instructions, the judge is required to do all except which of the following:

    a.   Go over the testimony and tell the jury which evidence was more believable than other evidence.

    b.   Tell them the law that they should apply to the facts.

    c.   Specify the kind of verdict to be used.

    d.   Define which issues are to be determined.

10. _____   Appeals courts can issue:

       a.   Majority opinions.

       b.   Dissenting opinions.

       c.   Concurring opinions.

       d.   Remands.

       e.   All of the above.

MATCHING

Match the following terms or phrases to the descriptions below.

a.   New Maine National Bank v. Nemon

b.   Preponderance of the evidence

c.   Counterclaim

d.   Motion for judgment on the pleadings

e.   Request for admission

f.   Motion for summary judgment

g.   Voir dire

h.   Judgment notwithstanding the verdict

i.   Adversary system of justice

j.   Affirmative defense

k.   Reply

l.   Pleadings

m.   Discovery stage

n.   Deposition

o.   Judgment of the court

p.   Wauchop v. Domino's Pizza, Inc.

q.   Seventh Amendment of the U.S. Constitution

r.   May v. Hall County Improvement Association

s.   Complaint

t.   Pleadings

1. _____   In this case, an appellate court refused to dismiss an action against a corporate officer/director for failure to comply with discovery orders.

2. _____   Filed when there are no facts in dispute and asks the court simply to apply the law to those facts and resolve the dispute.

3. _____   The final resolution of a dispute unless there is an appeal.

4. _____   This is used to force admissions of facts about which there are no real disputes between the parties.

5. _____   If the challenging party had previously moved for a directed verdict, then after the verdict, it can file this motion.

6. _____   Their purpose is to notify each of the parties of the claims, defenses, and counterclaims of the adversary parties.

7. _____   This pleading is filed in those situations where the defendant files a counterclaim and the plaintiff elects to respond.

8. _____   In this pleading a defendant can deny allegations and assert his or her own claim against the plaintiff.

9. _____   In a civil trial, this burden of persuasion is required of the plaintiff to prove his or her contentions.

10._____   In answering the complaint, the defendant may admit to the plaintiff's allegations but may assert additional facts that will result in the action being dismissed.

11._____   Contains a statement alleging the facts necessary for the court to take jurisdiction, a short statement of facts necessary to show plaintiff is entitled to a remedy, and a statement of the remedy plaintiff is seeking.

12._____   It reflects the American belief that truth is best discovered through the presentation of competing ideas.

13._____   This case deals with contempt of a writ of execution.

14._____   This motion is essentially the same as a motion to dismiss, but it occurs after the pleadings have been completed.

15._____   During this stage, the parties are allowed to use a variety of procedural devices to obtain information and gather evidence about the dispute.

16._____   In this case, the court sustained a motion for a directed verdict.

17._____   The principal discovery tool, it is the sworn testimony of a witness recorded by a court official.

18._____   Provides for the right of a jury in a civil dispute.

19._____   The screening process used in selection the jury members, conducted either by the attorneys or the judge.

20._____   This stage involves the complaint, the answer, and the reply.

CASE PROBLEMS

1. Spillman was injured by a car driven negligently by Goodman, an AIDS victim. Spillman is concerned about Goodman's being available for trial, and she would like to get information about his insurance, his assets, and his driving record. What should she do?

    _____

    _____

    _____

2. Andrews is being sued by Phelps. He believes that they agree on some of the facts and that there is no factual dispute as to some of the issues in the lawsuit, merely a dispute as to the applicable law. What should he do?

    _____

    _____

    _____

3. A jury in southern California came in with a verdict for $16 million against the Ford Motor Co. as the result of a plaintiff's injuries suffered when the fuel tank of his Pinto blew up. What can Ford do?

    _____

    _____

    _____

4. Boyington is being sued by Conrad. Boyington is convinced that Conrad has done certain things that, if presented to the jury, would help Boyington. How can Boyington get at this information and at information certain witnesses have?

    _____

    _____

    _____

5.   Flour Mill has an outstanding judgment against City Bakery, which City refuses to pay. The issue of whether City owes the debt has already been litigated. What can Flour Mill do to collect the debt?

_____

_____

_____

APPLICATION QUESTIONS

DO YOU AGREE OR DISAGREE WITH THE FOLLOWING STATEMENTS? JOT DOWN YOUR REASONS.

1.. When Ross Perot wanted to sue General Motors for breach of contract, his attorneys filed a request to depose Chairman Roger Smith regarding his personal involvement with Perot's association with GM. Smith does not want to be forced to answer Perot's questions, so he defends on the grounds that the request is merely for harassment. Is this a valid defense?

Yes_____   No_____

Reasons:

2.   Ann was a member of a civil trial jury on a breach of contract claim. The plaintiff was female, the defendant male. Bill, the foreman of the jury, felt strongly that the defendant was not liable. He said so aggressively throughout the jury deliberations. He referred to the plaintiff as a "blood sucker," a "skin flint," and a "bitch." Ann was offended and felt that justice had miscarried when the jury ultimately released the defendant. Does she have legal grounds for complaint?

Yes_____   No_____

Reasons:

3.   The appellate court panel is troubled by the briefs they have read on <u>Smith v. Jones</u>. Questions remain as to the facts, the correct use of law by the trial judge, and the application of the law to the facts. Can they have the opposing attorneys present oral argument in addition to the briefs already filed?

Yes_____   No_____

Reasons:

4.   Bobby's Supply Co. has almost $300,000 dollars in accounts receivables against Noah's Ship Yard, and needs the cash badly. Noah's has been a good customer for the last fifteen years, but has recently fallen on hard times. Bobby is considering filing suit against Noah for the money. He should consider the company's good will in the community as well as whether the controversy is the kind for which the law furnishes relief.

Agree_____   Disagree_____

Reasons:

5.   De Costa has been sued for breach of contract by Harkinson, and has received the complaint through service of process. However, he does not believe that Harkinson has stated a claim that shows him to be entitled to a legal remedy. His first response in the pleading is a motion for summary judgment.

Agree_____   Disagree_____

Reasons:

CH. 4 - Alternative Dispute Resolution

OVERVIEW AND CHAPTER OUTLINE

This chapter considers negotiation, mediation, arbitration, and other forms of alternative dispute resolution (ADR). It also addresses the use of judicial pressure on parties to resolve disputes before trial.

I. **ARBITRATION**

    A.   International Perspectives: Europe Emerges as the Arbitration Forum of Choice

    B.   The Arbitration Process

        1.   Selection of Arbitrators

        2.   The Hearing

        3.   The Award

        4.   Appealing the Award

        5.   Juris*prudence*? Arbitrate or Take a Beating?

    C.   Voluntary and Compulsory Arbitration

        1.   Public Sector Employment

3.   Proposed Changes to the Federal Rules of Civil Procedure

4.   State Changes to Encourage ADR

D.   Advantages of ADR to Businesses

V.   SUMMARY

VI.   ISSUE: WILL THERE BE ANY CASES LEFT FOR THE COURTS?

KEY WORDS AND PHRASES

Alternative dispute resolution (ADR)   Court annexed arbitration
Arbitration   Res judicata
Arbitrator   Negotiation
Submission   Mediation
Award   Minitrial
Federal Arbitration Act (FAA)   Summary jury trial

FILL-INS

1. _____   Disputant control is greatest in this type of dispute resolution process.

2. _____   This is the most widely recognized form of ADR.

3. _____   This is what the arbitrator's decision is called.

4. _____   This process begins the arbitration proceedings.

5. _____   These international rules for effective arbitration have become the statutory model in several European countries.

6. _____   This statute of Congress requires that agreements to arbitrate must be honored.

7. _____   This process, which is usually mandatory, requires arbitration as a pretrial requirement.

8. _____   This kind of ADR is available in most states to resolve disputes involving public sector employees.

9. _____   The proper name for the New York Convention.

10._____   The least formal form of ADR.

11._____   A form of negotiation usually less rigid than arbitration.

12._____   A negotiation strategy that involves making only one settlement offer.

13._____   The neutral third party facilitator in mediation.

14._____   An organization that helps train and credentialize mediators.

15._____   A structured settlement process that can blend negotiation, mediation, and arbitration.

16._____   This is the jury equivalent of a minitrial.

17._____   ADR processes are guaranteed this, as are other pre-trial settlement activities.

18._____   This Congressional legislation requires every federal court to study and develop a caseload management plan.

19._____   This Act of Congress requires all federal agencies to adopt an ADR policy.

20._____   This state requires all attorneys to advise clients about the use of ADR techniques.

MULTIPLE CHOICE QUESTIONS

Select the best answer to each of the following questions.

1. _____   Arbitration is:

    a.   Always binding.

    b.   Another word for mediation.

    c.   An alternative method of dispute resolution.

    d.   Only used in labor-management disputes.

2. _____   Arbitrators, when resolving legal disputes:

    a.   Are bound by stare decisis.

    b.   Conduct hearings which are less formal than trials.

    c.   Take part in conducting the voir dire of prospective jurors.

    d.   Cannot take part in the voir dire of jurors being impaneled to hear the case.

    e.   Must be attorneys.

3. _____   In Cincinnati Gas and Electric Co. v. General Electric Co., the court found that:

    a.   Summary jury trials are settlement procedures.

    b.   The First Amendment right of access historically does not apply to settlements.

    c.   Summary jury trials are so similar to trials that they may be treated as trial by the press.

    d.   All of the above.

    e.   A and b only.

4. _____   Alternative Dispute Resolution may provide which of the following:

    a.   Mini-trials.

    b.   Negotiation.

    c.   Mediation.

    d.   Summary Trials.

    e.   All of the above.

5. _____   The U.S. Supreme Court's holding in <u>Gilmer v. Interstate / Johnson Lane Corp.</u>:

    a.   Cited with approval the Federal Arbitration Act's public policy of favoring arbitration agreements.

    b.   Held that arbitration agreements between brokerage houses and employees did not violate public policy.

    c.   Has expanded the use of arbitration in statutory claims.

    d.   All of the above.

    e.   A and b only.

6. _____   Which of the following is <u>not</u> true?

    a.   Chief Justice Warren Burger said litigation takes business managers away from creative development and production.

    b.   The courts are generally hostile to ADR.

    c.   Ousted business executives often prefer unfair dismissal litigation to ADR.

    d.   All of the above.

    e.   B, c, and d.

7. _____   International commercial disputes:

    a.   Are increasingly arbitrated.

    b.   May result in awards that cannot be enforced.

    c.   Are mandatory under the U.N. Commission on International Trade Law

    d.   All of the above.

    e.   A and b only.

8. _____   Arbitration:

    a.   Must be a voluntary agreement among parties in the private sector.

    b.   May be compulsory for public sector employment issues.

    c.   Must be conducted by arbitrators who are experts in the field and are attorneys or retired judges.

    d.   All of the above.

    e.   A and b only.

9. _____   Certain ethical norms apply to ADR including:

    a.   The neutrality of the arbitrator or mediator.

    b.   The duty not to defraud another through misrepresenting the truth.

    c.   Confidentiality of negotiations.

    d.   All of the above.

    e.   A and c only.

10. ____   The Ford Mediation Program:

   a.   Is binding on both dealers and consumers if they first both agree to mediate.

   b.   Is binding only on Ford and its dealers.

   c.   Denies dealers the due process of a trial with a jury.

   d.   All of the above.

   e.   B and c only.

MATCHING

Match the following terms or phrases to the descriptions below.

a.   London Court of International Arbitration

b.   Federal Arbitration Act

c.   Hoosac Tunnel Dock and Elevator Co. v. O'Brien

d.   Merrill Lynch v. Bobker

e.   American Arbitration Association

f.   Gilmer v. Interstate / Johnson Lane Corp.

g.   NLRB v. Joseph Macaluso

h.   "Information exchange"

i.   "Court-supervised" minitrial

j.   Summary jury trial

k.   In re NLO, Inc.

l.   Judicial Improvements Act of 1990

m.   Administrative Dispute Resolution Act of 1990

n.   Clinton's Executive Order (1996)

o.   Pretrial conference

p.   Wrongful dismissals

q.   Panels

r.   Stock broker - customer arbitral agreements

s.   Medical malpractice

t.   Texaco - Borden dispute

1. _____   This is the jury equivalent of a minitrial, after discovery has been completed.

2. _____   This meeting of judge and opposing counsel before litigation is designed to settle the issues in dispute.

3. _____   This dispute over a huge antitrust claim was settled soon after a minitrial.

4. _____   Many states require these claims to be arbitrated, to help constrain health costs.

5. _____   This law gives federal district courts wide latitude in reducing caseload through use of ADR.

6. _____   One of Europe's best private organizations for providing fair arbitration standards and process in international business disputes.

7. _____   These suits are often brought by salaried highly placed business managers when they loose their jobs.

8. _____   These agreements often keep disputes over securities accounts from being tried before juries.

9. _____   This case permitted an arbitral award to be overturned where the arbitrator's error was obvious to the average person qualified to serve as an arbitrator.

10. _____   This Act permits the EPA to settle environmental disputes with ADR.

11. _____   This case upheld the freedom of mediators to avoid subpoenas as witnesses in litigation subsequent to the mediated dispute.

12. _____   This federal statute makes written contractual agreements to arbitrate compulsory and enforceable at law.

13. _____   A group of up to three arbitrators, agreed on by the parties, to hear the dispute.

14. _____   This case required a federal district court to vacate an order to compel parties to conduct a public, summary jury trial.

15. _____   A hearing in which attorneys from both disputants summarize the dispute for senior executives from each party.

16. _____   The President required the use of binding arbitration by federal agencies in expanded circumstances.

17. _____   This private professional organization provides standardized "submissions" for arbitration.

18. _____   This case extended judicial immunity to arbitrators to protect them from undue influence and insure their impartiality.

19. _____   This case upheld compulsory arbitration of employment disputes under the rules of the New York Stock Exchange.

20. _____   This format was adopted by the federal district court in Massachusetts to mange a complex lengthy patent / antitrust case.

CASE PROBLEMS

1.   Thom's Peanuts has a dispute with South Georgia Peanut Cooperative over the quality of peanuts produced under contract. The claim could be tried by federal district court, or it could be negotiated. Which choice gives Thom's more control?

_____

_____

_____

2.   If Thom's claim arises under a contract with an arbitration agreement, can Thom insist on a trial?

_____

_____

_____

3.   If Thom's arbitrates the claim, does it have any choice in an arbitrator?

_____

_____

4.   If the arbitrator refuses to hear evidence about Thom's other peanut contracts, entered with other peanut producers, is this a ground for overturning the arbitral award?

_____

_____

_____

5.   If Thom's goes to trial to enforce payment of the arbitral award, will the court allow him to state a cause of action?

_____

_____

_____

APPLICATION QUESTIONS

DO YOU AGREE OR DISAGREE WITH THE FOLLOWING STATEMENTS?   JOT
DOWN YOUR REASONS.

1.   Cannon Manufacturing Company entered into a contract with Ammunition Supply
      House, which included a clause in which both parties agreed to submit any
      controversies to binding arbitration.   After Ammunition supplied defective goods, and
      refused to replace them with correct supplies, Cannon brought suit against Ammunition
      for damages arising from breach of contract.   Can Ammunition force Cannon to go
      before an arbitrator, rather than a judge?

      Yes_____   No_____

      Reasons:

2.   Little Old Lady Lila put her life savings into an account with Milkim and Howe, an
      investment firm.   The contract included a clause that provided that in the event of a
      dispute, the parties agreed to submit binding arbitration.   Mr. Milkim absconded with
      Miss Lila's money, and she wants to sue him for breach of contract and punitive
      damages.   Must she honor the arbitration clause first?

      Yes_____   No_____

      Reasons:

3.   Vic Victim has a disputed claim with Good Samaritan Insurance Company.   He is
      willing to mediate but not arbitrate.   He believes he will maintain more flexibility in
      mediation.

      Agree_____   Disagree_____

      Reasons:

4. Dick Doctor sues Past Partners over misuse of partnership funds, and the court orders a minitrial as part of a pretrial settlement. Dick would agree to the minitrial, but he wants it closed to the public. Can he insist on this?

    Yes_____   No_____

    Reasons:

5. The Federal Mediation and Conciliation Service provides mediators for union-management contract disputes, most of which are resolved. When disputes cannot be resolved before trial, can FM&CS mediators be subpoenaed to testify at trial?

    Yes_____   No_____

    Reasons:

CH. 5 - Business and the Constitution

OVERVIEW AND CHAPTER OUTLINE

This chapter discusses the various constitutional provisions that impact business and gives specific examples of how these prohibitions and protections operate to protect or deter business activities.

I.   **THE COMMERCE CLAUSE**

    A.   The Necessary and Proper Clause

        1.   <u>McCulloch v. Maryland</u>

        2.   Federal Supremacy

    B.   Defining "Commerce" Among the Several States

    C.   Interstate Commerce Broadly Defined

    D.   Federal/State Regulatory Relations

        1.   When State Law Impedes Interstate Commerce

        2.   Juris*prudence*? Great Constitutional Moments

II. **THE TAXING POWER**

    A. Federal Taxation

    B. State Taxation

        1. Apportioning State Tax Burden

        2. State Taxes May Not Impede Foreign Trade

III. **BUSINESS AND FREE SPEECH**

    A. Business and Political Speech

    B. Business and Commercial Speech

        1. Juris*prudence*? Don't Care for the Book, Huh?

        2. Speech and Competition

        3. Freedom to Criticize

IV. **OTHER KEY PARTS OF THE BILL OF RIGHTS**

    A. Unreasonable Search and Seizure

        1. Limits on Searches and Inspections

        2. Restrictions on Use of Evidence

        3. International Perspectives: Constitutional Law in Foreign Jurisdictions

    B. Self-incrimination

    C. Just Compensation

        1. Regulatory Takings

    D. Right to Trial

    E. Excessive Fines

V. **FOURTEENTH AMENDMENT**

A.   Due Process

    1.   Juris*prudence*? No Hammer Locks, Ladies

B.   Equal Protection

VI.   **SUMMARY**

VII.   **ISSUE: SHOULD FREE SPEECH RIGHTS APPLY AT THE WORKPLACE?**

KEY WORDS AND PHRASES

U.S. Constitution
Commercial speech
Preamble
Political speech
Federal judiciary
Unreasonable search and seizure
Bill of Rights
Commerce Clause
Fourth Amendment
Interstate commerce
Warrantless searches
Intrastate commerce
Self-incrimination
Supremacy clause

Excessive fines
Necessary and proper clause
Fifth Amendment
Federal preemption
Just compensation
Takings clause
Fourteenth Amendment
Due process clause
Taxing power
Freedom of speech
Right to trial
Exclusionary rule
Closely regulated industry
Equal Protection clause

FILL-INS

1. _____   When Congress has done this, the states have no power to regulate.

2. _____   Provides that no person shall be compelled in any criminal case to be a witness against himself.

3. _____   Addresses the rights of persons to trial by jury in criminal cases.

4. _____   Is a powerful device for extending federal constitutional guarantees to the states and preventing states from passing laws that diminish any federal constitutional protections.

5. _____   The Fifth Amendment does not prohibit the taking of private property, but requires that this be given if such property is taken.

6. _____   This clause, along with the commerce clause, has been held to provide justification for broad congressional control of commerce.

7. _____   The decision in <u>Marshall v. Barlow's, Inc</u>. restricted these.

8. _____   Until recently, they had broad powers to change zoning and land use requirements without paying compensation, even though the value of the land may be affected by the change in land use rules.

9. _____   If it passes a regulation that is constitutional, the states may not pass regulations that would impede the effect of the federal rule.

10. _____   Prohibits the use of evidence gathered by law enforcement officials in a manner that violates Fourth Amendment rights.

11. _____   This case held that it was a violation of due process to bring within a state's jurisdiction a foreign corporation that had no agents in the state, made no direct sales there, and did not design or distribute the final product for commerce there.

12. _____   These exclusions of persons on a jury may not be race based.

13. _____   In the Michigan Chamber of Commerce case, the U. S. Supreme Court upheld limitations on this kind of corporate speech.

14. _____   This case held that a state bar association may not prohibit the truthful advertising of legal services through letters to individual clients.

15. _____   May be subject to federal governance only to assist in the regulation of interstate commerce.

16. _____   Provides that no state can deny equal protection of the law.

17._____   While these cannot be forced to testify against themselves, they can be forced to produce business records that might incriminate the corporation (and executives), since such records are not protected by the Fifth Amendment.

18._____   Has been interpreted to give Congress the power to enact most of the federal regulation of business.

19._____   Takes precedence over state regulation that directly contradicts or reduces the standards imposed by federal law.

20._____   Provides for the right to jury trial in common law cases.

MULTIPLE CHOICE QUESTIONS

Select the best answer to each of the following questions.

1. _____   Which of the following is not one of the seven Articles that make up the Constitution?

    a.   Method for ratifying the Constitution.

    b.   Methods for amending the Constitution.

    c.   Creation of a taxing agency.

    d.   Creation and powers of the federal judiciary.

2. _____   The U.S. Constitution:

    a.   Consists of five articles and the Bill of Rights.

    b.   Includes the Bill of Rights even though it is actually an act of Congress and is not an amendment.

    c.   Like the British constitution, consists of well established traditions rather than a written document.

    d.   Consists of 7 articles and 27 amendments.

3. _____   Assume that a state on the west coast prohibits commercial fishing in its coastal waters by nonresidents. A federal statute licenses commercial fishing vessels for operations in coastal waters. The state statute is:

   a.   Valid under "the new federalism."

   b.   Invalid under the contract clause.

   c.   Valid as a legitimate exercise of a state's inherent power to enact legislation for the benefit of its citizens.

   d.   Invalid under the supremacy clause of the U.S. Constitution.

4. _____   Which of the following reflects the view of Constitutional doctrine expressed by Justice Story in Martin v. Hunter's Lessee?:

   a.   The Constitution was intentionally written in vague terms so as to give great discretion to the Congress.

   b.   The Constitution provides for minute specifications of its powers and processes.

   c.   Any decision by a state court must include appropriate federal law as the law of a state.

   d.   It is unconstitutional for a federal agency to issue an executive order.

5. _____   The commerce clause of the U.S. Constitution provides that "Congress shall have the power to regulate commerce with foreign nations and among the several states and with the Indian tribes." This federal power:

   a.   Has the effect of preempting all state authority over commercial activity.

   b.   Applies only to interstate commerce or international commerce and not to intrastate commerce.

   c.   Does not apply to any intrastate commerce even though it has a substantial effect on interstate commerce.

   d.   Has been liberally interpreted to give Congress extensive authority to regulate economic activity.

6. _____   The Bill of Rights consists of the first ten amendments to the U.S. Constitution. These amendments provide a set of fundamental rights that:

    a.   Do not apply expressly or directly to state governments. State citizens must look to their own state constitutions for guarantees of rights that are enumerated in the Bill of Rights.

    b.   Apply directly and expressly to the federal government and are fully incorporated into the Fourteenth Amendment's due process clause which is directly applicable to the states.

    c.   Apply directly and expressly to the federal government only.

    d.   Apply directly and expressly to both the federal and state governments.

7. _____   Freedom of the press is guaranteed in the U.S. Constitution. This basic right has been interpreted:

    a.   To permit one to yell "fire" in a theater.

    b.   To impose a different standard of liability in defamation cases brought against public figures.

    c.   To prohibit the government from making any restrictions on commercial speech.

    d.   To give an absolute right to newspapers to print anything about anyone no matter how libelous because it is important in a democracy to have a press that is not fearful of lawsuits for publishing stories.

8. _____   Congress enacted a statute regulating the size, design, and movement of oil tankers. A state also enacted a statute covering the same matters with regard to oil tankers operating in its waters. The state restrictions were more strict than were the federal ones. Several oil companies sued the state, asserting that the restrictions were unconstitutional. Which of the following should the court use in resolving the conflict?

   a.   The commerce clause.

   b,   The fourteenth amendment.

   c.   The first amendment.

   d.   The preemption doctrine.

9. _____   The federal taxing power permits the federal government to obtain revenue to support its operation. Which of the following is a correct statement about this power?

   a.   Taxation is an insignificant regulatory tool.

   b.   Taxpayers have no standing to sue the government because they feel their tax rate is too high.

   c.   Taxation of income from interstate commerce by state and local governments does not conflict with the commerce clause.

   d.   Taxation is a means of implementing social policy.

10. _____   A state statute declared the advertising of the price of a prescription drug by a licensed pharmacist to be nonprofessional conduct. This statute was:

   a.   Upheld because commercial speech is unprotected by the first Amendment.

   b.   Upheld as a reasonable exercise of the due process power.

   c.   Struck down because commercial speech is protected to the same extent as noncommercial speech.

   d.   Struck down because commercial speech is protected if it concerns lawful activity and is not misleading.

MATCHING

Match the following terms or phrases to the descriptions below.

a.   BMW of North America v. Gore

b.   Commercial speech

c.   Marshall v. Barlow's. Inc.

d.   New York v. Burger

e.   Asahi Metal Industry Company v. Superior Court of California

f.   Necessary and proper clause

g.   Browning-Ferris Industries of Vermont v. Kelco Disposal

h.   Nolan v. California Coastal Commission

i.   Southern Pacific Co. v. Arizona

j.   Martin v. Hunter's Lessee

k.   Gibbons v. Ogden

l.   Hughes v. Oklahoma

m.   Wickard v. Filburn

n.   Sonzinski v. U.S.

o.   Perez v. U.S.

p.   Katzenbach v. McClung

q.   Tull v. U.S.

r.   Consolidated Edison Co. v. Public Service Com.

s.   Shapero v. Kentucky Bar Association

t.   South-Central Timber Development Inc. v. Wunnicke

u.   <u>Dolan v. City of Tigard</u>

1. _____   This case discussed the general language of the Constitution and the ability of Congress to use that language to "mold and model the exercise of its powers, as its own wisdom and the public interest should require."

2. _____   This clause gives Congress the power to deal with matters beyond the list of specified federal concerns as long as control of those matters will help Congress be more effective in executing control over specified concerns.

3. _____   This case upheld a New York statute allowing warrantless searches of junkyards because such statutes are needed to inspect businesses that are subject to close regulations.

4. _____   In this case the Supreme Court struck down an Arizona statute that, for safety considerations, required trains to be shorter in Arizona than in other states.

5. _____   This case held that courts are not free to speculate as to the motives which moved Congress to impose federal taxing schemes.

6. _____   This case held that when the legal issue in a case is close to that of a common law right, jury trial rights exist.

7. _____   This case restricted the power of a state agency to require a private landowner to grant public access to beach front property as a condition to receiving permission to build a larger home on the property.

8. _____   This case held that a state could not enact legislation suppressing inserts in utility bills that discuss controversial public issues because it directly infringes on the freedom of speech protected by the First Amendment.

9. _____   This case held that the Due Process clause in the Fourteenth Amendment can be violated by "grossly excessive" punitive damages.

10. _____   This case used the commerce clause to extend nondiscrimination requirements of the 1964 Civil Rights Act to essentially local operations.

11. _____   This case held that commerce among the states means "commerce which concerns more states than one."

12. _____   This case held that the assertion of jurisdiction over a foreign businessman through the use of the state's long arm statute violated the protections provided by the Fourteenth Amendment.

13. _____   This case held that, in cases where state regulation of natural resources impacts interstate commerce, the regulation must be designed to have minimum impact.

14. _____   This case held that there can be no limitations on punitive damages under the Eighth Amendment between private parties in a civil case.

15. _____   This case upheld Congressional regulation of credit markets including federal regulation of local loan sharking activities.

16. _____   This case struck down an Alaska requirement that timber cut on state lands be processed within the state before export.

17. _____   This case held that bar associations could not prohibit truthful solicitations for legal services.

18. _____   A public expression related solely to the economic interests of the speaker and its audience.

19. _____   This case held that OSHA inspectors could not conduct warrantless searches of a business.

20. _____   This case held that federal controls on the production of wheat applied to small farms because, while one farmer would not make a difference, all the small farmers added together would have a substantial impact on the wheat market.

21. _____   This case held that a local ordinance requiring public use of private property in exchange for a building permit was a "taking" which required compensation.

CASE PROBLEMS

1.   Unlike all other states in the West and Midwest, Iowa prohibited by statute the use of 65-foot double trailer trucks within its borders. Consolidated Freightways owned 65-foot trailers which it was prohibited from using to carry commodities through Iowa on interstate highways. In a suit by Consolidated, should the statute be declared unconstitutional?

_____

_____

_____

2.   The Little Bit of Heaven delicatessen has received an order from Food and Drug Administration to close its business because of unsanitary conditions, grading the quality of the building and the store's products. The owners now want to stay open, satisfied that they have complied with the FDA requirements. May they seek a determination of this issue in the court?

_____

_____

_____

3.   Williams took over as editor-in-chief of the Herald Press, a biweekly small town newspaper and began exposing scandals in state government. The state passed a statute creating a Commission to censor all new state publications. Williams claims this is a violation of her constitutional rights. Is she correct?

_____

_____

_____

4. An electronic poker club has been using billboard advertising for its games, but has incited the wrath of local politicians who want to stop this gambling activity. They want to pass an ordinance restricting poker advertisements from billboards and other public displays, confining them to newspapers, and to the owner's storefront property. Can this be done under the rationale in Central Hudson?

5. The School Board of Washington, D. C., conducted warrantless searches of all school bus drivers, by requiring random urine tests for evidence of alcohol or drug use. Is this permissible under Skinner v. Railway Labor Executive Association?

APPLICATION QUESTIONS

DO YOU AGREE OR DISAGREE WITH THE FOLLOWING STATEMENTS? JOT DOWN YOUR REASONS.

1. When Billy's beach lot is rezoned by the state for environmental protection measures, so that he no longer has the right to build a vacation house on it, he has a constitutional right to be paid the fair market value of the property.

    Agree_____   Disagree_____

    Reasons:

2.   The state of Georgia passed a law that radioactive wastes from the Savannah River Plant in South Carolina could not be driven directly through the city of Atlanta on the way to a dump site, although that was the shortest and least costly route. Georgia's regulation would be upheld for "safety considerations" under the precedent in <u>Southern Pacific Co. v. Arizona.</u>

Agree_____   Disagree_____

Reasons:

3   Hawaii passed a 3% tax on all tourists coming into the state, which exempted Hawaiian business travelers. Hawaii claims the tax is necessary to pay for airport and harbor expenses connected with the tourist industry. This is constitutional.

Agree_____   Disagree_____

Reasons:

4.   Last Chance Bank wants to support its president in his campaign for mayor in Sleepy Hollow, and includes his political brochures in its customers' monthly statements. Orth Opponent is one of the Bank's customers, and takes umbrage at this use of the Bank's mailing. He can successfully petition the Court to make the Bank stop this practice.

Agree_____   Disagree_____

Reasons:

5.   Shanghai Corporation, located in Indonesia, has filled an order for crock pot thermostats, to be used in crock pots assembled in Mexico, and sold in the United States. When one of the crock pots explodes and the manufacturer is sued in a products liability action in Kentucky, it wants to counter claim against Shanghai for the defective part. Under the "due process clause," the manufacturer can force Shanghai to come to the United States to defend.

Agree_____   Disagree_____

Reasons:

CH. 6 - Government Agencies and Administrative Process

OVERVIEW AND CHAPTER OUTLINE

This chapter reviews the nature of administrative agencies and the administrative process. It begins with the development of administrative agencies in the U.S. The chapter then explores the legislative, investigative, adjudicatory, and enforcement powers of the agencies, and the right of judicial review. The chapter concludes with a discussion of Congressional limitations on the agencies.

I. **ADMINISTRATIVE AGENCIES**

    A.   Creating An Administrative Agency

        1.   Why Create an Agency?

    B.   Administrative Law

    C.   Rulemaking

    D.   Types of Rules

        1.   Juris*prudence*? Just in Case You Were Not Sure

        2.   Substantive Legislative Rules

KEY WORDS AND PHRASES

Administrative agency	Judicial review
Legislative delegation	Procedural requirements
Enabling statute	Standing
Rulemaking	Actual cases or controversies
Substantive rules	Ripeness doctrine
Interpretative rules	Exhaustion doctrine
General policy statements	Scope of review
<u>Federal Register</u>	Arbitrary, capricious,
Procedural rules	or an abuse of discretion
Subpoena	Sunset provisions
Sanction	Legislative vetoes
Informal procedures	Cost-benefit analysis
Formal procedures	Privacy Act
Adjudicatory hearing	Government in the Sunshine Act
Administrative law judge	

FILL-INS

1. _____ A formal process involving the agency and an individual or a small group of individuals.

2. _____ Authority given to an agency to assure that it has the ability to implement the statutory responsibilities delegated to it by Congress.

3. _____ Because of the rising complexity of regulatory matters and the large number of industry activities that come under regulatory supervision, agencies increasingly require businesses to do this.

4. _____ This can be defined as an authority of the government -- other than a legislature or a court -- created to administer a particular legislative enactment.

5. _____ This law requires Congress periodically to review an agency's regulations, programs, or general usefulness.

6. _____ This act of Congress delegates powers to an agency.

7. _____   The test for this is whether the agency decision or action challenged has caused the party seeking review some injury in fact, economic or otherwise, and whether the interest sought to be protected falls within the zone of interests to be governed by the statute in question.

8. _____   Consists of those legal rules that define the authority and structure of administrative agencies, specify an agency's procedural formalities, and define the roles of the courts and other governmental bodies in their relationships with agencies.

9. _____   This requires an administrative agency to undertake an analysis of all regulations it promulgates, and if costs exceed benefits derived from a regulation, the regulation would be eliminated or scaled down.

10. _____   They have become the primary tool through which local, state, and federal governments perform virtually all of their regulatory functions.

11. _____   This requires that all documents submitted to or held by federal agencies be made available to the general public.

12. _____   The agency's function is to assure protection of the environment by a systematic abatement and control of pollution.

13. _____   Through these procedures, the agency seeks formally to develop administrative rules and to articulate its regulatory policy.

14. _____   These rules are used to establish an agency's organization, describe its method of operation, and detail its internal practices.

15. _____   Statements issued by an agency to provide both its staff and the public with guidelines regarding the interpretation of a particular statute or regulation within the scope of its regulatory responsibility.

16. _____   This is the primary act of Congress establishing procedures for federal agencies.

17. _____   Is the congressional authorization to perform its specific regulatory purpose and to formulate appropriate public policy.

18. _____   This law is intended to give citizens more control over what information is collected about them and how that information is used.

19. _____   The agency's function is to insure just and equitable enforcement of occupational health and safety standards.

20. _____   Administrative agency laws or statutes with the same force and effect of law as statutes enacted by Congress.

MULTIPLE CHOICE QUESTIONS

Select the best answer to each of the following questions.

1. _____   A description of an administrative agency is that it is a government board, commission, office, bureau, or department:

   a.   Whose primary authority is enforcing law.

   b.   Housed only within the executive branch of the federal or a state government.

   c.   Independent of the executive, legislative, or judicial branches of government.

   d.   With power to make rules and adjudicate disputes affecting private rights.

2. _____   Rulemaking by an administrative body:

   a.   Is required to meet the same rigid procedural standards as adjudication.

   b.   At the federal level, is subject to the APA.

   c.   Is not governed by the APA.

   d.   Does not involve public proceedings.

3. _____   In general, federal administrative agencies may exercise:

      a.   Judicial power only.

      b.   Legislative power only.

      c.   Executive power only.

      d.   Executive, judicial, and legislative power.

      e.   Judicial and legislative power only.

4. _____   Federal regulatory agencies do not have power to:

      a.   Investigate violations of statutes and rules.

      b.   Prosecute violations of statutes and rules.

      c.   Impose criminal sanctions on violators.

      d.   Conduct hearings and decide whether violations have occurred.

5. _____   In reviewing an administrative agency's decision, a court will generally:

      a.   Make its own independent determinations of fact.

      b.   Accept jurisdiction whether or not all administrative appeals have been exhausted.

      c.   Make a redetermination as to the credibility of witnesses who testified before the agency.

      d.   Affirm the decision of the agency if it is both reasonable and rational.

6. _____   Administrative law is:

    a.   The substantive law produced by an administrative agency.

    b.   Found only in statutes.

    c.   Produced only be an independent legislative agency.

    d.   Any law regarding the powers and procedures of an administrative agency.

7. _____   Which of the following is a correct statement about legislative and interpretative rules issued by an administrative agency?

    a.   Interpretative rules are not subject to judicial review.

    b.   The making of interpretative rules is subject to the notice and public participation requirements.

    c.   The making of legislative rules is subject to the notice and public participation requirements.

    d.   Legislative rules are not subject to judicial review.

    e.   None of the above is correct.

8. _____   Judicial review of an administrative action:

    a.   Is permitted at any time during the administrative process.

    b.   Is subject to the exhaustion and ripeness doctrines.

    c.   Is generally unavailable.

    d.   Is available only if the agency agrees.

    e.   Is limited only to cases and not administrative actions.

9. _____   Suppose an FTC examiner concludes that Johnson has violated the FTC Act and made adverse determinations on several issues. Johnson:

    a.   Must accept the determination unless she was denied due process.

    b.   Should go to state court to reopen the case.

    c.   Must exhaust available administrative remedies before relief in court can be sought.

    d.   Can ignore the hearing because such delegation of power to the FTC would be invalid.

10. _____   Which of the following powers do administrative agencies not have?

    a.   Rulemaking powers.

    b.   Adjudication.

    c.   To bring actions in state courts to enforce their adjudication decisions.

    d.   Investigation.

MATCHING

Match the following terms or phrase to the descriptions below.

a.   Atlas Roofing Company, Inc. v. Occupational Safety and Health Review Commission

b.   Critical Mass Energy Project v. Nuclear Regulatory Commission

c.   the Federal Register

d.   Administrative law judges

e.   Interpretative rules

f.   United Technologies v. EPA

g.   Clean Air Act

h.   Subpoena

i.   <u>Dow Chemical Company v. U S.</u>

j.   Adjudication

k.   Sunshine Act

l.   <u>FTC v. Ruberoid Company</u>

m.   Judicial review

n.   Informal agency procedures

o.   Administrative Procedures Act

p.   Exhaustion doctrine

q.   Formal agency procedures

r.   <u>Georgia Pacific v. OSHA</u>

s.   Occupational Safety and Health Agency

t.   Administrative agency

1. _____   This act entitles the public to at least one week's notice of the time, place, and subject matter of any agency meeting, and notice of whether the meeting is to be open or closed to the public.

2. _____   An administrative agency's counterpart to a judicial trial.

3. _____   This case held that an interpretative rule intends to set forth what the agency thinks a statute means, while a legislative rule intends to create new legal rights and duties from that statute.

4. _____   They range from informal general policy statements to authoritative rules that are binding on the agency.

5. _____   This doctrine holds that parties may appeal agency decisions into federal courts.

6. _____ This agency has been accused of being ineffective in protecting workers, although it had severe cutbacks by the executive branch in the 1980's.

7. _____ In this case, Justice Jackson, in the dissent, said that administrative agencies have become the fourth branch of the government, which has deranged all our three-branch legal theories.

8. _____ This case held that courts are willing to overturn an agency's regulatory discretion, and even, to a lesser extent, its interpretive discretion.

9. _____ Because of their nature, they lie outside the procedural controls provided by the APA, thereby allowing considerable agency discretion in forcing compliance.

10. _____ This is typically initiated by the filing of a complaint by the agency against a business whose behavior is in question.

11. _____ The most fundamental administrative law.

12. _____ This case held that the Seventh Amendment's right to a jury trial is not required in agency adjudicatory hearings.

13. _____ It is created by Congress when a problem is perceived as requiring a considerable degree of expertise, flexibility, and continuous supervision in working toward solutions.

14. _____ A Congressional enactment that provides that a business may be required to monitor its air pollution and report the data to the EPA.

15. _____ This legal instrument orders the recipient to testify or produce documents.

16. _____ This requires a party to complete agency review procedures before appealing to a court.

17. _____ This case held that a warrantless search was permitted when investigators flew over a plant and took pictures.

18. _____ These are administrative hearing officers who render written decisions.

19. _____ This is the official government document in which agencies must publish all proposed rules.

20. _____ This case held that agency disclosure of certain reports may not be compelled under the Freedom of Information Act.

CASE PROBLEMS

1. The Secretary of Commerce issued a standard on flammability that required all mattresses, including crib mattresses, to pass a test that involved contact with a burning cigarette. Manufacturers of crib mattresses petitioned the court to excuse crib mattresses from the flammability standard. They claimed that the action was arbitrary and capricious since infants do not smoke. How should the court rule?

    _____

    _____

    _____

2. Adams Brewery is accused of price fixing by the FTC. After a complete adjudicatory hearing, the Commission concluded that Adams has in fact engaged in illegal price fixing. Substantial evidence was presented at the hearing in support of the Commission's finding. But Adams also presented substantial evidence that it had never entered into any price-fixing arrangements. Should a reviewing court uphold the FTC's findings?

    _____

    _____

    _____

3. Section 553 of the APA prescribes the procedures agencies must follow in rulemaking proceedings. A court decided that the proceedings before a federal agency were inadequate and overturned a rule. This decision was reached despite the fact that the agency employed all the procedures required by Section 553. How would the Supreme Court rule on the question of whether courts are free to require agencies to follow additional rulemaking procedures?

    _____

    _____

    _____

4.   The President campaigned on the promise that he would get government off the backs of businesses, and now he asks your advice on how to do this. He wants you to offer concrete suggestions on how to free businesses from the arrogance and burden of dealing with OSHA, and all those troublesome workers who spend their time complaining rather than working as they should. What can you tell him?

_____

_____

_____

APPLICATION QUESTIONS

DO YOU AGREE OR DISAGREE WITH THE FOLLOWING STATEMENTS? JOT DOWN YOUR REASONS.

1   The bank investigators were of such poor quality in the S & L industry in the 1980's that they did not know there were bad business practices in the making of loans until depositors began pulling out their accounts in 1987.

      Agree_____   Disagree_____

      Reasons:

2.   Kennedy's Meat Packing Company was inspected by a team from OSHA, who found health and safety violations. It is not legal for the agency to threaten public exposure of the violations in order to force the Company to correct the violations.

      Agree_____   Disagree_____

      Reasons:

3.   Acme Toy Company reads in the <u>Federal Register</u> that the Federal Consumer Product Safety Commission has proposed a new rule that would ban all toys that were painted with lead-based paint, because of its toxicity when digested by humans. Acme has just purchased 500 gallons of paint, which is lead based, and does not want to lose money by scrapping it. Acme's only hope of relief is to bring suit immediately in federal court.

Agree_____   Disagree_____

Reasons:

4.   Paul's Package Shop may be required to file quarterly reports showing whether or not it has complied with administrative agency regulations. If the agency determines from the reports that Paul's has not complied with regulations, it may penalize the Shop. This is unconstitutional under the Fifth Amendment protections against self-incrimination.

Agree_____   Disagree_____

Reasons:

5.   The Federal Communications Commission intends to restrict the height of private radio antennas, to the distress of the Ham Radio Operators Association. One of their members suggests that they lobby Congress to cut back on funding for the FCC, if the agency enforces the rule. This is neither legal nor ethical.

Agree_____   Disagree_____

Reasons:

CH. 7 - Torts

OVERVIEW AND CHAPTER OUTLINE

This chapter discusses tort liability, and how that liability affects the business community. It distinguishes and defines the relationship among intentional torts against persons and against property, the torts of negligence, and the torts of strict liability.

I. **THE SCOPE OF TORT LAW**

    A.   Role of Tort Law

    B.   Business and Torts

    C.   Costs of Tort Litigation

II. **INTENTIONAL TORTS AGAINST PERSONS**

    A.   Establishing Intent

        1.   Business Liability

    B.   Assault

    C.   Battery

        1.   Assault and Battery

        2.   Defenses

4.   Substantial Factor

D.   Defenses to a Negligence Action

1.   Assumption of Risk

2.   Comparative Negligence

V.   STRICT LIABILITY

A.   Ultrahazardous Activity

VI.   SUMMARY

VII.   ISSUE: ARE GREEDY CONSUMERS CAUSING THE PUNITIVE DAMAGE "CRISIS"?

KEY WORDS AND PHRASES

Tort
Intervening conduct
Tort feasor
Intent
Willful misconduct
Law of Agency
Superseding cause
Intentional torts
Assumption of risk
Assault
Affirmative defense
Battery
Defense
"But for" (sine qua non) rule
Consent
Comparative negligence
Privilege
Self-defense
"Danger invites rescue"
False imprisonment
The "Reasonable Person" test
Antishoplifting statutes

Substantial factor test
Legal cause rule
Invasion of privacy
Strict liability
Ultrahazardous activity
Punitive damages
Defamation
Slander
Libel
Defamation per se
Absolute privilege
Conditional privilege
Constitutional privilege
Truth
Actual malice
Malicious prosecution
Infliction of emotional distress
Real property
Personal property
Misappropriation
Quasi-delit
Unreasonable

Risk of harm   Public nuisance
Ordinary care   Private nuisance
Due care   Trespass to personal property
Causation   Conversion
Foreseeable   Negligence
Trespass to land   Proximate cause rule

FILL-INS

1. _____   Is the intentional detention of an individual within boundaries if that individual knows about the detention or is harmed by it.

2. _____   Is an activity that substantially and unreasonably interferes with the use and enjoyment of the land or an interest in the land of another.

3. _____   This occurs when statements are made that are presumed by the law to be harmful to the individual to whom they were directed and, therefore, require no proof of physical harm or injury.

4. _____   A rule that may hold a defendant liable who creates such a dangerous situation that the plaintiff is rescued by someone else who is also harmed.

5. _____   The test used to determine whether the defendant acted carefully or negligently.

6. _____   This new rule is a substitute for the old rule of proximate causation.

7. _____   A tort which imposes liability without fault.

8. _____   Is an unlawful touching, a direct and intentional physical contact without consent.

9. _____   This tort involves intentional conduct by an individual that is so reckless or outrageous it creates severe mental or emotional distress in another.

10. _____   This consists of an unlawful invasion of the property of another.

11. _____   Is a civil wrong, other than a breach of contract, for which the law provides a remedy.

12. _____   Is an intentional false communication that injures an individual's reputation or good name.

13. _____   This tort may occur by an appropriation of an individual's name or picture without permission or by a public exposure of facts that are private in nature.

14. _____   This element of proof characterizing conduct which the defendant knows, or should know, will likely result in injury.

15. _____   This element must be proven to hold liable members of the press who publish defamatory material written about public officials or public figures.

16. _____   This is an absolute defense to the tort of defamation.

17. _____   Is the intentional conduct directed at a person by an individual that places that person in apprehension of immediate bodily harm or offensive conduct.

18. _____   Under this rule, damages are reduced by the percentage of injuries caused by the plaintiff's own negligence.

19. _____   An unreasonable interference with a right held in common by the general public.

20. _____   Is an intentional and wrongful interference with possession of personal property of another without consent.

MULTIPLE CHOICE QUESTIONS

Select the best answer to each of the following.

1._____   A tort is:

    a.   A breach of contract.

    b.   A crime.

    c.   A violation of the Constitution.

    d.   A harm caused by socially unreasonable conduct.

2._____   Which of the following is an essential element of the tort of assault?

    a.   The injured party's awareness of the defendant's conduct.

    b.   Harmful or offensive touching of the body.

    c.   The defendant's intent to cause a battery.

    d.   Actual danger of bodily harm.

3._____   Which of the following is an essential element of the tort of defamation?

    a.   Intentional communication of a false statement.

    b.   A writing.

    c.   Publication to a third party.

    d.   A tape recording.

4._____   In what way is criminal law most distinguishable from tort law?

    a.   The criminal defendant is presumed innocent until proven guilty.

    b.   A crime is a violation of public law and is prosecuted in the name of the state.

    c.   Punishment of a crime may be by imposition of a fine.

    d.   A criminal defendant is presumed guilty until proven innocent.

5._____   The Long Island Railroad was not liable to Mrs. Palsgraff because:

    a.   It was only liable to the passenger with the explosives for willful misconduct.

    b.   Its negligence was not the proximate cause of her injury.

    c.   The explosion was set off by a passenger, not by a railroad employee.

    d.   There was a "but for" relationship between the explosion and the act of pushing the passenger onto the moving train.

6._____   Arthur heard a noise in his carport, looked out, and saw a man trying to break into his car. Which of the following is not legal?

    a.   He may use whatever force is reasonable to protect his property.

    b.   He may threaten to call the police and have the man arrested.

    c.   He may threaten to shoot the thief.

    d.   He may fire his gun at or near the thief in an effort to frighten him away.

7._____   Personal property is:

    a.   Something which is not real property but is firmly attached to the land.

    b.   Immovable.

    c.   Something capable of being owned that is not real property.

    d.   Minerals in the land.

8._____   While shopping with his mother at the supermarket, fourteen-year old Ronald dropped a banana peel on the floor in the produce department. Three hours later, Mort, a customer, slipped on the peel and broke his leg. Which of the following is correct?

    a.   Mort cannot collect from the store but must sue Ronald.

    b.   Mort cannot collect from the store but can only recover from Ronald's mother.

    c.   Mort can recover from the Supermarket only if it can prove that the store had actual notice that the banana peel was on the floor.

    d.   Mort can probably recover from Supermarket if it failed to inspect and clear the floor within a reasonable time.

9._____   Traditionally, a plaintiff in an action for the tort of negligence must prove that:

    a.   The defendant intended to injure the plaintiff.

    b.   The instrumentality causing the harm was abnormally dangerous.

    c.   The defendant's action proximately caused injury to the plaintiff.

    d.   The defendant acted with gross negligence and in willful, wanton, and reckless disregard of the welfare of the plaintiff.

10._____   In which of the following cases is the plaintiff most likely to prevail in a suit for infliction of emotional distress?

    a.   The defendant's conduct is so outrageous as to cause severe mental anguish.

    b.   The defendant's conduct involves ultrahazardous activity.

    c.   The defendant's conduct is crude and rude to the plaintiff.

    d.   All of the above.

MATCHING

Match the following terms or phrases to the descriptions below.

a.   Palsgraf v. Long Island Railroad Company

b.   Wassell v. Adams

c.   Substantial factor

d.   Crump v. P & C Food Markets

e.   Battery

f.   Privilege

g.   Judge Cardoza

h.   Caldwell v. K-mart

i.   Fust v. Francois

j.   Defamation

k.   Infliction of emotional distress

l.   Funeral Services by Gregory, Inc. v. Bluefield Community Hospital

m.   Bethlehem Steel v. Ernst & Whinney

n.   False imprisonment

o.   Peoples Bank and Trust v. Globe International

p.   Pendoley v. Ferreira

q.   Trespass

r.   Assault

s.   White v. Monsanto Co.

t.   Tort

1. _____   This "legal cause rule" will permit a finding of liability even if the defendant's action was only one important element in causing the plaintiff's harm.

2. _____   A civil wrong, other than a breach of contract for which the law provides a remedy.

3. _____   This case held that when one brings suit against another without a reasonable belief in the validity of complaint under law, malicious prosecution may be found.

4. _____   In this case, the Jury used the comparative negligence doctrine to determine the relative fault of the young woman and the motel owner for the attack which she suffered.

5. _____   In this case, the court agreed with the jury verdict for a woman unreasonably restrained as a suspected shoplifter.

6. _____   In this case, the court refused to find that a battery had occurred because there was no intent on the defendant's part, and no physical injury to the plaintiff.

7. _____   This case held that the defendant had unreasonably interfered with the enjoyment of property of others, by continuing to operate a piggery.

8. _____   This case held that damages could be recovered where the defendant invaded the plaintiff's privacy by placing her in a false light.

9. _____   This tort involves the unauthorized intrusion of a person or thing on to the land of another.

10. _____   In this case, the court affirmed the grant of a new trial for an accounting firm charged with negligent preparation of an audit.

11. _____   This case held that there was defamation where an employer improperly called an employee a thief and fired him.

12. _____   This case held that where rude conduct fails to rise to the level of outrageous conduct, this tort for mental harm will not lie.

13. _____   Intentional detention of an individual within boundaries if that individual knows about the detention or is harmed by it.

14. _____   Intentional false communication that injures an individual's reputation or good name.

15. _____   Intentional conduct directed at a person by an individual that places that person in apprehension of immediate bodily harm or offensive conduct.

16. _____   A right to an immunity from liability.

17. _____   An unlawful touching, a direct and physical contact without consent.

18. _____   In a classic case, this judge held that because the injury to the plaintiff was not foreseeable, the defendant was not liable to her.

19. _____   Intentional conduct by an individual that is so reckless or outrageous it creates severe mental or emotional distress in another.

20. _____   This case is the landmark decision for any discussion and application of the concept of proximate cause.

CASE PROBLEMS

1. Bees-B-Ded Pest Control Company carefully fumigated the Courthouse each month. In May, last year, the chemicals caused the employees to have respiratory problems so badly that the Courthouse had to be evacuated. Could Bees-B-Ded be liable for any damages even though they were not careless?

    _____

    _____

    _____

2. Dalton suffered electrical burns when a tool he was using to clean a chicken feed bin contacted overhead high-voltage power lines owned by Habersham Electric Membership Corp. Habersham knew the feed bins were constructed under the power lines, and three wires did not meet the clearance requirements of the National Electric Safety Code. Dalton sued Habersham for negligent construction and maintenance of the power lines. Will he prevail? Explain.

    _____

    _____

    _____

3. Bernie, senior partner in the accounting firm of Beanne and Counter, undertook to advise a limited partnership on its tax matters, to prepare its books and tax returns, and to issue financial reports to its investors. In recording a charitable donation which involved a gift of property to a hospital, Bernie forgot to reduce the value of the gift by the amount of "relief of indebtedness," in other words, by the amount of the outstanding mortgage on the property which the hospital agreed to pay off on behalf of the partnership. This mistake cost the partnership significantly more taxes and penalties when it was discovered on an IRS audit than the property had been worth in the first place. The partners want to sue the accountant for the harm that he has caused them. What is their cause of action, and what elements must they prove to prevail?

    _____

    _____

    _____

4. Paper Goods, Inc. sought punitive damages from Party Goods, Inc. for unlawfully using Paper Goods distinctive colorful store decor. Since the plaintiff is a business, and businesses protest high tort damage awards by juries in personal injury cases, will the court allow Paper Goods to claim punitives?

_____

_____

_____

5. A barge was tied to a pier in a midwest city near the Great Lakes in March, a time when the ice in the river was beginning to break up and flow down stream. The night watchman had left the barge to go to a cafe for coffee when the moorings broke loose, and the barge was thrust downstream by the flowing ice. It careened into the side of a neighboring barge, tore it loose also, and the two barges slammed into a bridge about a half-mile further down the river. The bridge was severely damaged, and two cars which were then crossing the bridge were thrown into the river. One person was killed and another seriously injured. Can the victims and their representatives bring an action against the owner of the first barge? What is that defendant's best defense? What does this have to do with Mrs. Palsgraff?

_____

_____

_____

APPLICATION QUESTIONS

DO YOU AGREE OR DISAGREE WITH THE FOLLOWING STATEMENTS? JOT DOWN YOUR REASONS.

1.   Sarah meant to slap Frank's face when he made a leering and sexually offensive comment to her, but her fingernail hit his eyeball when he jumped away from her. His eye was severely damaged, and he sues her for his damages from personal injury. She admits the act, but defends saying that she did not intend to harm him, only to rebuff his advances. She is not liable to Frank.

       Agree_____   Disagree_____

       Reasons:

2.   Michael's business had suffered from a rash of burglaries, so he installed a metal grid over the front door and plate glass window, electrified it, and posted warning notices saying that the electricity was working. Gabriel intended to break in to the store, but avoided the metal grid, climbing up on the roof to enter through the air conditioning vent. When he made contact with the metal vent, he was electrocuted, because an electrical short had occurred in the fuse box between the grid outlet and the a. c. system. Michael did not know that this had happened. Gabriel's widow sued Michael for his death, claiming that Michael had set a spring gun in violation of the law. Michael should not be liable for Gabriel's death.

       Agree_____   Disagree_____

       Reasons:

3.   Charlie backs over Fred in the parking lot of the Twist and Shout Nightclub, after a drinking session. Fred can sue Charlie in tort for personal injury and the state can prosecute Charlie for the crime of D. U. I., without putting Charlie in double jeopardy.

Agree_____   Disagree_____

Reasons:

4.   Roy was mad with Madeline, so he told Madeline that her son had just been killed by a runaway truck. Madeline screamed in horror, and had a heart attack. Roy was just joking, and never had any idea that Madeline would suffer physical injury. She does not have a good cause of action against him for intentional infliction of emotional distress.

Agree_____   Disagree_____

Reasons:

5.   When Nellie inadvertently dropped her blood pressure medicine in Molly's iced tea, and Sarah drank the tea and fainted, knocking over the lamp which cut Barbara's hand, Nellie was not liable to Barbara in that Barbara was not a foreseeable victim.

Agree_____   Disagree_____

Reasons:

CH. 8 - Business Torts

OVERVIEW AND CHAPTER OUTLINE

This chapter focuses on the areas of tort law that are of particular concern to businesses. It examines disparagement, defamation, interference with contracts of other businesses, and premises liability. It also traces the evolution of the law of product liability from the theory of caveat emptor through the development of negligence standards to the era of strict liability.

I.   **TORT LAW AND BUSINESS**

      A.   Disparagement

      B.   Employee Defamation

      C.   Interference with Contractual Relations

      D.   Interference with Prospective Advantage

      E.   Premises Liability

II.   **PRODUCT LIABILITY**

      A.   International Perspective: Is Japan Really Different?

KEY WORDS AND PHRASES

Disparagement
Intentional interference with
   contractual relations
Interference with prospective advantage
Predatory behavior
Premises liability
Privity of contract
Product misrepresentation
Negligence
Defenses
Caveat Emptor
Strict liability in tort
American Law Institute
Reasonable care
Second Restatement of Torts

Strict liability
Failure to warn
Design defects
Foreseeable event
Unknown hazards
Warranty theory
Implied warranty
Joint and several liability
Express warranty
Market share liability
Implied warranty of safety
Product misuse
Assumption of the risk
Sophisticated purchaser defense

FILL-INS

1. _____   This tort arises when an untrue statement is published about a business or its dealings and convinces others not to deal with that business.

2. _____   Refers to the relationship that exists between two contracting parties.

3. _____   To recover under this tort theory the injured party must prove that the business breached the duty to warn of unexpected dangers.

4. _____   Rule that requires the buyer to examine, judge, and test a product for himself.

5. _____   Duty owed by the manufacturer of a product to consumers, measured by the probability and cost of harm.

6. _____   This tort involves a wrongdoer who willfully causes another to break a good contract with competing business.

7. _____   Under this theory of liability, a manufacturer is required to exercise reasonable care in the production of its product where there are foreseeable dangers.

8. _____   Under this theory, manufacturers are required to pay compensation to consumers injured by defective products even though the manufacturer exercised all reasonable care.

9. _____   Adoption of strict liability by this body in its Second Restatement of Torts spurred the adoption of strict liability in tort in product-related injury cases throughout the country.

10. _____   This liability theory is based on the relationship between the injured party and the manufacturer as dictated by the existence of a warranty.

11. _____   A warranty which the law derives by an implication or inference from the nature of the transaction between the parties.

12. _____   This tort involves landlord liability for accidents that happen on their property.

13. _____   A consumer injury caused by a defective food or drink product constitutes a breach of this warranty.

14._____   Says that where a defect is not discoverable for many years after ingestion of a drug, and a victim cannot identify the manufacturer of the drug, the victim can sue all manufacturers and recover from them according to their percentage of the market for the drug.

15._____   Product abuse, assumption of the risk, and contributory negligence.

16._____   An implied promise by a merchant that a product is fit for the purposes for which it is being sold.

17._____   The UCC provides that this is created if a seller makes promises or statements about the product that become part of the basis of the bargain.

18._____   A defense theory used against products liability where the defective product was sold to a business experienced in dealing with the goods.

19._____   Theory of strict liability in which an Alaska court held a manufacturer of adult diet food liable where it failed to provide adequate warnings about using the diet food as baby food.

20._____   This applies when a person knows the risks associated with using a product, but continues to use the product, and is injured.

MULTIPLE CHOICE QUESTIONS

Select the best answer to each of the following questions.

1. _____   The concept of negligence law emerged to limit the liability of defendants in the nineteenth century. The twentieth century has seen the development of strict liability. Which of the following best states the basis of this current tort theory?

    a.   Liability based on intentional wrongdoing.

    b.   Liability without fault.

    c.   Products liability.

    d.   Liability based on fault regardless of intent.

2. _____   A plaintiff who is injured because a defective product was unreasonably dangerous may sue on the basis of negligence. Which of the following is not a possible obstacle to recovery?

     a.   Defendant raises the defense of assumption of risk.

     b.   Defendant raises the defense that s/he exercised all reasonable care.

     c.   The parties are not in privity.

     d.   Defendant raises the defense of contributory negligence.

3. _____   Jones is suing the manufacturer, the wholesaler, and the retailer for bodily injuries caused by a lawnmower he had purchased. Under the theory of strict liability:

     a.   Contributory negligence on Jones' part will not be a bar to recovery.

     b.   The manufacturer can always avoid liability if it can show that it followed standard industry custom.

     c.   Jones can recover even though he cannot show that there was any negligence involved.

     d.   Privity may be a bar to recovery insofar as the wholesaler is concerned because the wholesaler did not have a reasonable opportunity to inspect.

4. _____   In order to win in a suit based on strict liability in tort, an injured person must show, among other things, that when the product left the manufacturer it was in a condition not contemplated by the ultimate purchaser- consumer that would make it unreasonably dangerous to her. "Unreasonably dangerous" means that the product was:

     a.   Defective.

     b.   Defective and inherently dangerous.

     c.   Dangerous beyond the reasonable expectation of an ordinary consumer.

     d.   Inherently dangerous.

5. _____   Unless specifically excluded, a contract for the sale of goods between a merchant and a consumer includes a warranty of:

    a.   Fairness.

    b.   Usefulness.

    c.   Adequate consideration.

    d.   Merchantability.

6. _____   The rule requiring privity of contract for the manufacturer to be liable to a consumer in the case of MacPherson v. Buick Motor Co. was:

    a.   Upheld.

    b.   Extended.

    c.   Overthrown in favor of strict tort liability.

    d.   Overthrown making the producer liable for negligence for certain dangerous products.

7. _____   Under strict liability, the seller of a product is not liable for injury:

    a.   Due clearly to misuse by the buyer.

    b.   Due to some idiosyncrasy or unusual susceptibility of the buyer.

    c.   If the seller warns the buyer that its use is entirely at buyer's risk.

    d.   If neither the seller or buyer foresaw the potential risk.

    e.   None of the above.

8. _____   In which of the following cases is the plaintiff most likely to prevail in a suit for intentional interference with contractual relations?

   a.   Defendant asks the third party to break a contract with the plaintiff to make a contract with the defendant.

   b.   Defendant asks the third party to do business with the defendant rather than doing business with the plaintiff.

   c.   Defendant pushes its advertisements on the third party who it knows to be doing business with the plaintiff.

   d.   All of the above.

9. _____   The American Law Institute recommended:

   a.   That products liability always follow a "looser pays" rule.

   b.   That no more damages for pain and suffering be awarded.

   c.   Compliance with government standards be a defense to liability.

   d.   All of the above.

10._____   Anderson suffered an injury caused by a malfunction of a power saw he had purchased from Phil's Hardware. The saw was manufactured by General Tool Co. Anderson has begun an action against Phil's and General Tool Co. based on strict liability. Which of the following is a correct statement?

   a.   The suit will be dismissed because strict liability has not been applied in product liability cases in the majority of jurisdictions.

   b.   General Tool Co. will not be liable if it manufactured the tool in a nonnegligent manner.

   c.   Privity will not be a valid defense against Anderson's suit.

   d.   Anderson's suit against Phil's will be dismissed since Phil's was not at fault.

MATCHING

Match the following terms or phrases to the descriptions below.

a.   <u>Menefee v. Columbia Broadcasting System</u>

b.   <u>MacPherson v. Buick</u>

c.   <u>Baxter International v. Morris</u>

d.   <u>Robi v. Five Platters, Inc.</u>

e.   <u>Monette v. Am-7-7 Baking Company, Ltd.</u>

f.   <u>Cipollone v. Liggett Group Inc.</u>

g.   <u>Sindell v. Abbott Laboratories</u>

h.   <u>Ann M. v. Pacific Plaza Shopping Center</u>

i.   Warranty of fitness for a particular purpose

j.   <u>Baxter v. Ford Motor Co.</u>

k.   <u>Pree v. The Brunswick Corp.</u>

l.   Strict liability

m.   <u>Mazzetti v. Armour</u>

n.   Design defect cases

o.   <u>Greenman v. Yuba Power Products</u>

p.   <u>Borel v. Fibreboard</u>

q.   <u>Collins v. Eli Lily Co.</u>

r.   Sophisticated purchaser

s.   <u>Hennigsen v. Bloomfield Motors</u>

t.   <u>Morales v. American Honda Motor Co.</u>

1. _____   This case affirmed an award of damages for intentional interference with contractual relations.

2. _____   This case differentiates between defamation of reputation and disparagement of a property interest.

3. _____   Permitted a DES victim to sue any or all manufacturers of the drug even though the victim did not know which particular company made the pills that directly caused her injuries.

4. _____   This case rejected the market share liability theory, but allowed joint and several liability.

5. _____   This case held that the defendant had intentionally interfered with the business relationship of another, by taking the plaintiff's customer list and using it improperly.

6. _____   Premises liability for failure to protect patrons and employees of shopping centers from criminal acts turns on the issue of foreseeability.

7. _____   Under this rule of strict liability for ultrahazardous activity, the actor is responsible for resulting injuries regardless of the level of care exercised.

8. _____   This case disregarded the privity of contract requirement and held a manufacturer of food implies the food's safety for human consumption through the act of selling it to the general public.

9. _____   A theory of defense which relieves businesses of the duty to warn about obvious dangers when a product is sold to another manufacturer.

10. _____   This case held both the manufacturer of a product and the dealer who sold it to the purchaser's wife (who was driving the automobile when the accident occurred) strictly liable for her injuries and damages on the basis of an implied warranty of safety.

11. _____   Arises in those instances where a seller knows the purpose to which the buyer intends to put the product, and the buyer relies on the seller's expertise to supply a suitable product.

12. _____   This court denied liability in a design defect case involving dangerous unguarded propellers where testimony indicated that guards could worsen injuries.

13. ____   Under this rule, an injured party is not required to attack the conduct of the manufacturer, but rather is required to attack the product.

14. ____   These cases do not concern individual products that slip through the production process with a defect, but concern cases where if the product had been designed differently it would have prevented a particular type of injury.

15. ____   In this case, the court elected to hold an asbestos manufacturer liable regardless of whether the manufacturer knew of the danger at the time the goods were placed in commerce but rather on the basis of what we know today about the dangers of the products because the product was inherently defective.

16. ____   This case struck down the privity rule and held a manufacturer liable for negligence for a product-related injury.

17. ____   This decision allowed both breach of express warranty and negligence to become bases of liability for smokers.

18. ____   Failure to warn may make a product unreasonably unsafe if the warnings fail to point out the specific dangers of misuse.

19. ____   This case reversed a lower court's decision which refused to allow advertising that claimed a windshield was shatterproof to be introduced in an action involving an eye injured when a pebble hit a windshield causing a small piece of glass to fly into the plaintiff's eye.

20. ____   This California case held for the first time that strict liability in tort was available for a product injury case.

CASE PROBLEMS

1. Carie Palmer, a twenty-four year old married woman, went to her doctor to obtain birth control therapy. After she rejected birth control pills because of their potential side affects, her doctor recommended the Dalcon Shield. Her decision was based on information provided by the manufacturer and the sales representatives of the Dalcon Shield and on her doctor's description of the Shield as a superior IUD, safer than birth control pills and 98.9% effective in preventing pregnancy. Although she was fitted with a Shield, she became pregnant, and developed a uterine infection that caused a miscarriage. As a result of the miscarriage, she went into septic shock from a massive infection and dangerously low blood pressure. She sued the manufacturer on the basis of negligence and strict liability. What must she prove to prevail?

    _____

    _____

    _____

2. Marine Manufacturing Co. was a manufacturer of engines for boats. It distributes these engines exclusively through franchise dealers. Marine realized that the fuel filter recommended for its engines would occasionally crack and rupture under pressure. After developing a new filter, Marine notified all of its franchisees of the new filter, told them to use them in the future, and warned them that if they installed the old filters there was a danger that the old filter could rupture causing fuel to spray over the engine. Boat Sales, Inc., a franchisee, received a copy of the letter but later sold an engine to Marco and installed an old filter in it. Boat Sales, Inc. did not tell Marco of the problem with the old filter nor tell him to use the new filter. Marco installed the engine in his boat, and, on the first voyage, the filter exploded; fuel spread throughout the engine room, and the boat burned and sank. Marco sued both Marine Manufacturing and Boat Sales in negligence and in strict liability in tort. What would be the result? Explain.

    _____

    _____

    _____

3.   Holly purchased from Store, Inc. a raw pork roast that was sliced into pork chops. Holly prepared them for the family dinner by frying them on both sides for fifteen minutes until browned, then adding water, putting a cover on the skillet and boiling them for an hour and ten minutes over medium heat. After eating them, Holly and others in the family contracted trichinosis, a disease caused by parasitic worms that are sometimes present in raw or undercooked pork. Although there is no method of detecting the presence of trichinae in raw pork, it is generally known that this parasite infests pork, and it is generally known that pork must be well cooked before being eaten. Thorough cooking at a temperature of 137 or more degrees Fahrenheit destroys the parasite and makes the meat safe for human consumption. Holly sues Store, Inc. based on strict liability. Should Holly prevail? Explain.

_____

_____

_____

4.   In the earliest strict product liability cases, such as <u>Greenman v. Yuba Power</u>, how did the court rationalize a finding of liability and therefore damages without finding "fault" or negligence?

_____

_____

_____

5.   Beverly Landrine sued on behalf of her deceased infant daughter who died after she swallowed a balloon while playing with a doll known as "Bubble Yum Baby." The doll could simulate the blowing of a bubble gum bubble by inserting a balloon into the doll's mouth and pumping the doll's arm. The balloon was manufactured by Perfect Products Co. and distributed by Mego Corp. The plaintiff claimed that the balloon was defectively made or inherently unsafe when used by children and that Mego Corp. failed to warn of dangers associated with the balloon's usage. Who should prevail? Why?

_____

_____

_____

APPLICATION QUESTIONS

DO YOU AGREE OR DISAGREE WITH THE FOLLOWING STATEMENTS? JOT DOWN
YOUR REASONS.

1.   Eve bought apples from Snake River Orchard, made them into apple butter, and sold
        them to a distributor who sold them to Adam's Grocery Store. There a jar was
        purchased by Cain who ate the apple butter and became deathly ill. His doctor said
        the apple butter was spoiled, causing him to suffer from food poisoning. Cain may sue
        Eve under a negligence standard without privity of contract.

        Agree_____   Disagree_____

        Reasons:

2.   Peter bought a motorcycle with leg guards. He removed the guards so as to cut down
        on wind resistance. He slid his bike on wet pavement, and ran under a truck,
        surviving the collision but losing his right leg. He has a good cause of action against
        the motorcycle maker for strict liability.

        Agree_____   Disagree_____

        Reasons:

3.   Shiner Eyeglass Manufacturing Company made and sold to High Flyer, a basketball player, a pair of goggles to cover his glasses while playing on the court. The goggles were designed to crack but not splinter on impact. Every hundredth pair was inspected as the glasses came off the assembly line. When High Flyer was wearing the glasses, Joe Jumper jumped for a shot, came down on top of High, and hit a hard right elbow into the goggles. The goggles shattered, and High lost an eye. Shiner is not liable for negligence of design.

Agree_____   Disagree_____

Reasons:

4.   Benjamin bought four General Firerok tires for his van, and set out on his vacation. The tires were warranted against blowout for 40,000 miles. Not ten miles from home, Benjamin was rear-ended by a truck, which spun his van around sideways. As he fought to regain control of the vehicle he heard the rear tire explode. The van tipped over on its side and broke Ben's back. He can sue General Firerok for breach of express warranty.

Agree_____   Disagree_____

Reasons:

5.   A number of textile mills make flannel cloth, which is widely used for children's sleep wear. Little Jamie was wearing a pair of flannel pajamas while he was toasting marshmallows in the fireplace on a winter evening. The pajamas suddenly ignited and burst into a ball of flame, burning him severely. His mother knew the retailer who sold her the pajamas but did not know the manufacturer. She may sue the retailer in strict liability, who may then bring suit against all the textile manufacturers according to their market share if the culpable manufacturer cannot be located.

Agree_____   Disagree_____

Reasons:

CH. 9 - Property

OVERVIEW AND CHAPTER OUTLINE

In this chapter we review the major forms of property: real property, personal property, and intellectual property. Property law determines the protected interests one has in certain property at common law and statutory law.

I. **REAL PROPERTY**

    A.   Historical Origins

    B.   Deeds and Titles

        1.   Rights Are Not Unlimited

    C.   Fee Simple

        1.   Evolving Property Law: Condominiums

    D.   Life Estates

    E.   Servitudes

        1.   Covenants

        2.   Easements

        3.   Adverse Possession

KEY WORDS AND PHRASES

Chattel	Tenant
Real property	Lease
Property	Liens
Deed	Eminent domain
Title	Police power
Estate	Zoning
Fee simple (absolute)	Intellectual property
Life Estate	Intangible property
Life Tenant	Infringement
Servitudes	Trademark
Covenant (running with the land)	Trade dress
Easement	Trade name
Profit	Copyrights
Easement by prescription	Service marks
Adverse possession	Fair use
Statutes of limitation	Patent
Leasehold	Trade secrets

FILL-INS

1. _____   Moveable personal property such as clothing and furniture.

2. _____   A legally protected expectation (right) to use the thing for one's advantage.

3. _____   A means by which the owner of a valid deed has legal possession of the property.

4. _____   The right to exclusive possession of an estate in land for an indefinite period of time, with the right of disposal.

5. _____   A right to enter and use land in possession of another.

6. _____   A binding promise that goes with an estate when it is transferred to a new owner.

7. _____   The right to remove valuable things from the estate of another.

8. _____   The use of the land of another without permission.

9. _____   One who has a legal interest in rented property for exclusive possession for a definite time.

10. _____   The right of the government to take private property for public use with just compensation.

11. _____   The right of the government to regulate the use of private land for the health or safety of the public.

12. _____   The right of the state to control the use of local land with regards to building size, quality, and type.

13. _____   The category of property produced by creative thinking.

14. _____   A commercial symbol (design, mark, logo, or word) that readily identifies goods in the marketplace.

15. _____   A commercial symbol of products and of service establishments (size, shape, color, texture, graphics, sales techniques) that is "inherently distinctive."

16. _____ The distinctive name of a company or business that can be protected at common law.

17. _____ Permitted copying of copyrighted works.

18. _____ A protective grant from the federal government securing an inventor's exclusive right to make, use and sell an invention for twenty years.

19. _____ A valuable piece of business information protected from public use.

20. _____ Wrongful unauthorized use of the intellectual property of another.

MULTIPLE CHOICE QUESTIONS

Select the best answer to each of the following questions.

1. _____ Although Microsoft and Coca-Cola are worth billions of dollars,

   a. Neither owns much real property.

   b. Both own private property.

   c. Both own intellectual property.

   d. Both enjoy federal property protection.

   e. All of the above.

2. _____   All of the following is true of real property <u>except</u>:

    a.   Real property includes land, things, growing on land, things attached to the land, and subsoil minerals.

    b.   Property rights can be exclusive and for an indefinite time.

    c.   Property rights can be restricted by common law and statutory law, as well as by the owner.

    d.   Property rights can be taken away from owners under government's powers of eminent domain without just compensation.

    e.   Restrictive building covenants are a kind of servitude on property rights.

3. _____   All of the following are kinds of property rights <u>except</u>:

    a.   Nuisances.

    b.   Easements.

    c.   Profits.

    d.   Tenancies.

    e.   Titles.

4. _____   In the <u>Hickerson v. Bender</u> case, the court held that:

    a.   The easement had been abandoned because the new owners had built on it.

    b.   The easement was subject to adverse possession because the building was actual, open and hostile.

    c.   The easement was subject to exclusive and continuous adverse possession for fifteen years.

    d.   The easement was not only abandoned but was also subject to adverse possession.

    e.   All of the above.

5. _____   A lease must contain all of the following <u>except</u>:

    a.   The identity of the parties.

    b.   The length of the lease.

    c.   The specific ending date.

    d.   The exact amount of rent.

    e.   A legal description or address of the premises.

6. _____   In <u>Barton v. Mitchell</u>, the tenant:

    a.   Proved a constructive eviction.

    b.   Broke the lease causing the landlord monetary damages.

    c.   Breached the covenant of quiet enjoyment.

    d.   Refused to hold the landlord harmless from claims of liability from "Body Electric."

    e.   All of the above.

7. _____   It is true that landlords:

    a.   Can evict tenants in the U.S.

    b.   Cannot evict tenants in Bombay.

    c.   Can raise rents in New York.

    d.   Will invest in new buildings in Manhattan but not in Bombay.

    e.   All of the above.

8. _____   Which of the following is <u>not</u> true?

    a.   The Lanham Act protects trademarks.

    b.   The Lanham Act protects authorship of books and music.

    c.   The Copyright Act protects commercial symbols printed on t-shirts.

    d.   All of the above.

    e.   B and c.

9. _____   In which of the following cases is the defendant most likely to prevail in a suit by a plaintiff for infringement of a trademark or trade name?

    a.   Defendant sells a soft drink called Coke.

    b.   Defendant sells a cough syrup called Smart's with a picture of two bearded men on the container.

    c.   Defendant sells a magazine called *Vogues*.

    d.   Defendant sells a beer it describes as "light" beer.

    e.   All of the above.

10. ____   All of the following are true of the Lanham Act <u>except</u>:

    a.   Protects the look and feel of products.

    b.   Protects sales techniques and services.

    c.   Does not protect trade names.

    d.   Protects trademarks.

    e.   Requires federal registration.

MATCHING

Match the following terms or phrases to the descriptions below.

a.   Rushing v. Mann

b.   Kohl v. U.S.

c.   Village of Euclid v. Ambler Realty

d.   Article I, Sec. 8, U.S. Constitution

e.   Hard Rock Cafe Licensing Corp. v. Concession Services, Inc.

f.   Two Pesos v. Taco Cabana

g.   Feist Publications v. Rural Telephone Service

h.   Lever Bros. v. U.S.A.

i.   Sony Corp. v. Universal City Studios

j.   Campbell v. Acuff-Rose Music Co.

k.   U.S. Gypsum Co. v. National Gypsum Co.

l.   TRIPS

m.   Buffets, Inc. v. Klinke

n.   Racing Strollers patent

o.   Feudalism

p.   Deed

q.   Condominiums

r.   Statutes of limitations

s.   Liens

t.   Suggestive marks

1. _____   The court held that protection through copyright was limited to original works.

2. _____   "Playing the Patent Game" can be too expensive a strategy for some companies fighting patent copycats.

3. _____   The writing that commonly transfers ownership of property.

4. _____   The court said the Lanham Act "bars the importation of [goods] bearing a trademark identical to a valid U.S. trademark."

5. _____   This case held that the will of Andrew Comer left the acreage to his heirs although he specifically did not name them in his will.

6. _____   The court held that private copying of copyrighted movies for personal use was a protected "fair use" exception to the Act.

7. _____   A system of property ownership in which all land was owned by the Crown and held by tenants and subtenants.

8. _____   This case noted that the right of eminent domain was always a right at common law, long before it was included in the Fifth Amendment of the U.S. Constitution.

9. _____   The Supreme Court held that parody of a musical work can be a "fair use" exception to the Copyright Act under some situations.

10._____   A fee simple estate for living space in a building with common or public areas owned by another.

11._____   This classic case held that zoning may restrict (and diminish) the value of private property without the owner being entitled to compensation.

12._____   Failure to disclose "the best mode" for carrying out the invention can result in loss of patent.

13._____   State laws setting lengths of time for certain causes of action, such as adverse possession.

14._____   Trademarks or trade names that hint at the product, while being creative.

15._____   This provides the basis for federal protection for intellectual property.

16._____   Trade-related aspects of intellectual property rights in the WTO.

17._____   Claims against property by creditors of the property owner(s).

18._____   The Lanham Act was interpreted to protect against counterfeit t-shirts.

19._____   Trade secrets cannot arise from recipes in the public domain.

20._____   The Lanham Act was interpreted to protect "trade dress" which included interior design and distinctive exterior decoration.

CASE PROBLEMS

1.   The Harmons have three adult children, one of whom has a physical handicap confining her to a wheelchair. It is expected that she will never marry. They want to protect her interests in their will, particularly as regards the home place, but they want their other children to receive interests in the home place too. Suggest a suitable property arrangement for them to establish in their wills.

_____

_____

_____

2.   Clyde has two residential lots at the beach, one on the beach front side of the road, and one directly behind it on the other side of the road. To maximize the value of the back lot, what kind of "servitudes" can he place on the beach front lot?

_____

_____

_____

3.   Susi owes Betty $7,000 for interior decorating work, which Betty has tried to collect unsuccessfully for over a year. Betty can't go into the house and remove her work, but she wants to force Susi to pay her. If she goes to court to collect her fees, what may she ask the court to order with regards to Susi's house?

_____

_____

_____

4.   Walt Disney has invested a great deal of money in Mickey Mouse as a symbol of its clean and wholesome family recreations service, and developed its theme parts around this image. If Barney the Dinosaur's creators wish to develop product lines and theme parks, what must they do to avoid charges of liability for intellectual property violations from Disney?

_____

_____

_____

5.   Paul invents a new surgical device that will decrease the loss of blood in liver transplant surgery, and he patents it. How can he protect his patent in other countries?

_____

_____

_____

APPLICATION QUESTIONS

DO YOU AGREE OR DISAGREE WITH THE FOLLOWING STATEMENTS? JOT DOWN YOUR REASONS.

1.   Property rights to ownership and / or use of land should change very slowly over time, if at all.

        Agree_____   Disagree_____

        Reasons:

2.   Frances rents a trailer to Jeff for a year's lease. During that time, the water hose behind the washing machine develops a leak. The drip falls on the floor, rotting the floorboard, so that the washing machine tilts down on the rotten board. Jeff can claim a "constructive eviction."

        Agree_____   Disagree_____

        Reasons:

3.   Loni has a new hair care product which she has patented and wants to sell, but she wants a special name for her product. "Loni's Locks" is one choice, but "Lovely" is another possibility. Is "Loni's Locks" a better choice?

        Yes_____   No_____

        Reasons:

4.   Hard Rock Cafe t-shirts abound with names of cities where no Hard Rock Cafe exists, yet the HRC design is clearly used.   Should the HRC pursue and prosecute the counterfeiters?

Yes_____   No_____

Reasons:

5.   A restaurant known as "Eat Your Vegetables" closes in Atlanta.   There is no other establishment by that name.   Is the name now available so that Dan can use it on his new dining establishment in Savannah?

Yes_____   No_____

Reasons:

CH. 10 - Contracts

OVERVIEW AND CHAPTER OUTLINE

This chapter begins with a discussion of the concept of freedom of contract and some limitations and restrictions on that freedom. It goes on to examine the sources of contract law, the elements of a contract, and concludes with an analysis of the ways in which a contract can be discharged, including remedies available to parties in the event of breach.

I. **DEFINITION AND CLASSIFICATIONS OF CONTRACTS**

    A.   Definition of a Contract

    B.   Classifications of Contracts

        1.   Express and Implied Contracts

        2.   Bilateral and Unilateral Contracts

        3.   Executory and Executed Contracts

        4.   Valid, Void, Voidable, and Unenforceable Contracts

        5.   International Perspectives: Contract Rights in Eastern Europe

        6.   Quasi-contracts

II. **ELEMENTS OF A CONTRACT**

A.   The Agreement

    1.   The Offer

        a.   Manifestation of Intent

        b.   Definite Terms and Conditions

        c.   Communication of the Offer

    2.   Terminating an Offer

        a.   Termination

        b.   Termination by the Parties

        c.   Termination by the Operation of Law

    3.   The Acceptance

        a.   Must Be Unconditional

        b.   Must Be Unequivocal

        c.   Must Be Legally Communicated

B.   Consideration

    1.   Adequacy of Consideration

    2.   Preexisting Obligations and Past Consideration

    3.   Settlement of Business Debts

        a.   Liquidated Debt

        b.   Unliquidated Debt

    4.   Juris*prudence*? If You Can't Trust A Lawyer

    5.   Enforceable Promises Without Consideration

C.   Capacity to Contract

        1.   Minors

        2.   Insane and Intoxicated Persons

   D.   Legality

        1.   Contracts Contrary to Public Policy

            a.   Exculpatory Agreements

            b.   Unconscionable Contracts

            c.   Contracts with Public Servants

            d.   Juris*prudence*? Life Just Isn't Worth Living

            e.   Contracts in Restraint of Trade

        2.   Effect of Illegal Agreements

   E.   Reality and Genuineness of Consent

   F.   Contracts in Writing and the Statute of Frauds

        1.   Sufficiency of the Writing

        2.   Parol Evidence Rule

III.   DISCHARGE OF CONTRACTS

   A.   Discharge by Performance

   B.   Discharge by Breach

        1.   Material Breach

        2.   Substantial Performance

        3.   Anticipatory Breach

   C.   Discharge by Condition

        1.   Failure of a Condition Precedent

     1.   Specific Performance

     2.   Injunction

V.   SUMMARY

VI.   ISSUE: SHOULD CONTRACT LAW BE AFFECTED BY TRADITIONAL BUSINESS PRACTICES?

KEY WORDS AND PHRASES

Contracts
Freedom of contract
Restatement of Contracts 2d
Uniform Commercial Code (UCC)
Promise
Express contract
Implied contract
Offeror
Offeree
Bilateral contract
Unilateral contract
Executory contracts
Executed contracts
Valid contract
Void contract
Voidable contract
Unenforceable contracts
Quasi-contract
Unjust enrichment
Agreement
Offer
Acceptance
Preliminary negotiations
Intent
Indefiniteness
Knowledge of the offer
Termination of an offer
Firm offers
Option contracts
Revocation

Counteroffer
Lapse of time
Intervening illegality
Death or insanity of
    the offeror or offeree
Mirror image
Printed-form contracts
Battle of forms
Mailbox rule
Performance
Consideration
Promisee
Promisor
Legal detriment
Legal benefit
Detriment-benefit test
Adequacy of consideration
Preexisting duty
Settlement agreement
Accord and satisfaction
Liquidated debt
Unliquidated debt
Promissory estoppel
    (or detrimental reliance)
Contractual capacity
Minor
Right to disaffirm
Nonvoidable contracts
Ratify
Intoxicated

Adjudicated insane
Insane in fact
Illegal bargain (or agreement)
Contrary to public policy
Exculpatory agreement
Unconscionable contracts
Covenant not to compete
Illegal agreements
Reality of consent (or genuine assent)
Meeting of the minds
Mutual mistake
Fraud
Deceit
Duress
Undue influence
Statute of frauds
Sufficient writing
Parol evidence rule
Discharge (of contract)
Breach of contract
Material breach

Substantial performance
Anticipatory breach (or repudiation)
Conditions (precedent, subsequent,
    concurrent)
Failure of a condition precedent
Express condition subsequent
Concurrent conditions
Discharge by legal impossibility
Objective impossibility
Subjective impossibility
Discharge by operation of law
Recision
Novation
Accord and satisfaction
Compensatory damages
Expectancy damages
Liquidated damages
Nominal damages
Punitive (or exemplary) damages
Special damages
Mitigation of damages
Equitable remedies
Specific performance
Injunction

FILL-INS

1. _____   These are valid contracts, but one of the parties to the contract has the right to avoid his/her obligation without incurring liability.

2. _____   A party's ability to perform legally valid acts, acquire legal rights, and incur legal liabilities.

3. _____   In this contract the parties do not state directly the promise or promises to one another, but rather the promises are inferred from the behavior of the parties or the circumstances in which they find themselves.

4. _____   This evolved from a 1677 English statute to prevent individuals from committing fraud by claiming that a contract was in existence when in fact it was not.

5. _____ This is formed when the offeree accepts the offer through an exchange of mutual promises.

6. _____ It was designed to bring the field of commercial law more in line with contemporary business practice and to promote uniformity of the laws relating to commercial transactions among the states.

7. _____ Business and economic historians have called this the fundamental and indispensable requisite to progress.

8. _____ This typically arises in contracts for the sale of a business and for employment, and the agreement is valid if reasonable, limited by time, and limited by territory.

9. _____ This subsequent illegality causes contracts that were once valid not to be enforced by the courts.

10. _____ It prohibits the introduction of oral evidence in a lawsuit where the evidence is contrary to the terms of a written contract.

11. _____ The offeree's expression of assent or agreement to the exact terms of the offer.

12. _____ This occurs when both parties agree that their contractual relationship should be terminated without performance.

13. _____ This occurs when the breaching party has deviated from the contract only slightly and not in bad faith.

14. _____ A contract that does not exist at law, such as a contract whose subject matter is illegal or a contract made by an individual without capacity to make a contract.

15. _____ This is formed when an offeree accepts an offer through an exchange of performance for the offeror's promise.

16. _____ These damages allow the plaintiff to receive relief beyond mere compensation, and are intended to deter wrongdoers from similar conduct in the future.

17. _____ Courts will not enforce these agreements, leaving the parties as they found them and not allowing the parties to recover damages for breach or for services already rendered.

18. _____   A contract created by a direct statement by the parties of a promise or promises to each other.

19. _____   These agreements release one party from the consequences brought about by his or her wrongful acts or negligence.

20. _____   Now in its second edition, it is an authoritative document that provides an orderly presentation and summary of the common law of contract.

MULTIPLE CHOICE QUESTIONS

Select the best answer to each of the following questions.

1. _____   In order to be valid, consideration must be:

    a.   Stated in the contract.

    b.   Based on a legal, as opposed to a moral, detriment.

    c.   Have a monetary value.

    d.   Be performed simultaneously by the parties.

2. _____   Salisbury promises Montana $1 million if Montana refrains from playing football for one year. Montana refrained and sued Salisbury for the $1 million when she refused to pay. Who will win?

    a.   Salisbury will win because she received no actual benefit.

    b.   Salisbury will win because Montana incurred no actual detriment.

    c.   Salisbury will win because Montana suffered no real detriment.

    d.   Montana will win because Salisbury received a legal benefit.

3. _____ Connors made an offer to pay Lloyd $5,000 if Lloyd would put on a tennis demonstration with him. Acceptance of Connor's offer occurs when Lloyd:

a. Prepares to perform.

b. Performs.

c. Promises to perform.

d. Goes to the club and buys a new tennis racket.

4. _____ In order for an offer to be effective, it must be:

a. Written.

b. Communicated.

c. Sent by telegram.

d. Sent by mail.

5. _____ Article 2 of the Uniform Commercial Code applies to contracts involving sales of:

a. Real Property.

b. Services.

c. Contractual rights.

d. Goods.

6. _____   Melli, a lawyer, sends a bill to Baylor for $10,000, for services as her attorney during a recent divorce. Baylor believes the amount is exorbitant and sends Melli a check for $8,500 and marks payment in full on the check. If Melli cashes the check, and later sues for the balance, she will:

    a.   Win because the debt is liquidated.

    b.   Lose because the debt is liquidated.

    c.   Lose because the unliquidated debt is now settled.

    d.   Win because the debt is unliquidated.

7. _____   Marshall is sixteen and goes to Smiling Jack's Used Car lot where she purchases a 1971 Volkswagen Bug for $6,000 ($4,000 over low Blue Book). When she takes the car for a drive the engine falls out. When she tries to rescind the contract, Smiling Jack refuses, saying that seventeen is almost eighteen, and Marshall looked eighteen. Who will win?

    a.   Smiling Jack because Marshall looked eighteen.

    b.   Smiling Jack because the law says "buyer beware."

    c.   Smiling Jack because anyone who deals with a used car dealer gets what s/he deserves.

    d.   Marshall because a minor can rescind most contracts.

8. _____   The statute of frauds makes certain agreements unenforceable unless they are:

    a.   Legal.

    b.   Not fraudulent.

    c.   Written.

    d.   Supported by consideration.

9. _____   An acceptance is generally effective when it is:

      a.   Received by the offeror.

      b.   Sent by the offeree.

      c.   Signed by the offeree.

      d.   Received by the offeree.

10. ____   Which of the following elements is not a requirement for a contract?

      a.   A writing.

      b.   Consideration.

      c.   Capacity.

      d.   Mutual assent.

MATCHING

Match the following terms or phrases to the descriptions below.

a.   Curtiss 1000 v. Suess

b.   Executory contracts

c.   Chang v. First Colonial Savings

d.   Discharge

e.   Restatement definition of a contract

f.   Valid contract

g.   Hamer v. Sidway

h.   Bradkin v. Leverton

i.   Hoffman v. Red Owl Stores

j.   Contract law

k.   Agreement

l.   Peevyhouse v. Garland Coal

m.   Blackstone's definition of a contract

n.   Busse v. Department of General Services

o.   Normile v. Miller

p.   Sherwood v. Walker

q.   Partially executed contracts

r.   Copenhaver v. Berryman

s.   Firm offer

t.   Unconscionable contract

1. _____   This case utilized the doctrine of promissory estoppel or detrimental reliance.

2. _____   An offer in writing specifying that the offer will remain open for a given time period and cannot be revoked until the stated time period expires.

3. _____   This occurs when the obligations of a contract are satisfied.

4. _____   This case held that quasi contracts are a mere fiction and are created by the law regardless of the intention of the parties to assure a just and equitable result.

5. _____   A promise or a set of promises for the breach of which the law gives a remedy, or the performance of which the law in some way recognizes as a duty.

6. _____   It is primarily state common law embodied in judicial opinions.

7. _____   This occur when one of the parties, being in a strong bargaining position, takes advantage of the other party and convinces him/her to enter into a contract contrary to his or her well-being.

8. _____   An agreement, upon sufficient consideration, to do or not to do a particular thing.

9. _____   This case considers the common law requirement of a "meeting of the minds" where a conditional acceptance becomes a counteroffer.

10. _____   This case held that recision was the appropriate remedy where the parties thought the cow was sterile, and she wasn't.

11. _____   Contracts that have not been fully performed by either party.

12. _____   A contract in which all the elements of a contract are present.

13. _____   This detriment or benefit test of consideration was used by the courts to impose obligations on one party to a dispute when to do otherwise would create an injustice to the other party.

14. _____   When a breach of contract occurs, the injured party is required to undertake reasonable efforts to mitigate damages or lessen the loss.

15. _____   An offer may be made by an advertisement if the terms show something definite was promised in positive terms for something requested.

16. _____   This means that there is a mutual understanding between the parties as to the substance of the contract, through an offer and acceptance.

17. _____   This contract has been fully performed by one party but not by the other.

18. _____   This case held that this covenant not to compete was invalid because the protected interest did not involve trade secrets, confidential information, or relations with "near-permanent" customers of the employer.

19. _____   This case refused to recognize a legal impossibility to allow a company to avoid its obligations to complete a construction job.

20. _____   This case discussed the calculation of damages for "an efficient breach" of contract.

CASE PROBLEMS

1. Bewley owned the Silver Spur Bar and hired Diana and Donald McNulty to operate it, promising them all bar revenues in excess of operating and fixed costs. Receiving virtually no income from the arrangement, the McNultys asked to be replaced immediately. Instead, Bewley offered them a 49% interest in the bar if they remained as managers for 2 additional years. They rejected the offer, but stayed on as managers for 14 months. They stated they continued working because Bewley promised to "make things right." At the end of 14 months, Bewley brought in a new manager, and the McNultys sued Bewley, alleging that a contract for reasonable wages was implied by law. Will they win?

    _____

    _____

    _____

2. Lyle School District sent a contract offer to Corcoran, a school teacher. The contract said that "If this contract is not signed and returned to the Secretary of the school district on or before June 14, 1976, the Board reserves the right to withdraw this offer."

    In addition, the superintendent of schools personally called Corcoran's attention to the time provisions in the contract. Corcoran did not return the signed contract until June 16. Two days later he received a letter from the superintendent stating that the board had decided not to accept any contracts returned after the June 14 deadline, and Corcoran was not rehired. He sued the school district. Who will prevail?

    _____

    _____

    _____

3.   Johnson owned real estate, and his real estate agent sent a letter to Mellen, indicating that certain seashore property that Mellen had expressed an interest in purchasing would be placed on the market. The letter said that several other people who had expressed an interest in the property were also being informed at the same time, before the property went on the open market. Mellen interpreted the letter as an offer and promptly accepted. When Johnson refused to sell him the property, Mellen sued. Was there a contract?

_____

_____

_____

4.   Fein was a prospective purchaser of a Budget Rent-A-Car franchise. Budget required prospective purchasers to sign an agreement requiring the prospective purchaser "not to enter into any daily discount automotive rental business in the western hemisphere for a period of two years" without written permission from Budget. He also agreed not to reveal any information about Budget's operations.

After signing the agreement, Budget divulged much confidential literature that Budget considered a trade secret. The deal fell through; Fein acquired another franchise of a competitor. Budget sued to enforce the covenant not to compete. Who will prevail?

_____

_____

_____

5.   Brighenti agreed to construct a building for Brian. After beginning construction, Brighenti discovered that a factory had previously been on the property and that a great deal of debris would have to be removed from the ground before construction could begin. Neither party had been aware of the subterranean debris, despite earlier test borings, and the contract did not contain a provision for cost of removing the debris. Brighenti refused to go on with the contract until they orally agreed that Brighenti would be paid all costs plus 10% for removing the unanticipated factory debris. After the work was completed, Brian refused to pay the added costs saying there was no consideration for the oral agreement, and Brighenti sued. Who will prevail?

_____

_____

_____

APPLICATION QUESTIONS

DO YOU AGREE OR DISAGREE WITH THE FOLLOWING STATEMENTS?   JOT DOWN YOUR REASONS.

1.   Luella has left her buggy at Lannie's Buggy Bath, with the keys in the ignition, and a message that she will be back in one hour. The employee decides to do more than merely wash the car for $5.00; he decides to give the car's engine a $30.00 steam cleaning job too. Under quasi-contract theory, Leulla is bound to pay for the car wash and the engine cleaning, so as to prevent "unjust enrichment."

Agree_____   Disagree_____

Reasons:

2.　Susan Solicitor is handling a real estate deal for Clara Client, and is involved in negotiations with Sarah Seller. Sarah offers a parcel of land for $87,000, which Clara tells Susan she will pay, but instructs Susan to try to bargain the price down if possible. Susan calls Sarah and tells her that $87,000 is too high, and says that Clara will pay $85,000. If it suits her purposes, Sarah treats that statement as a rejection and counteroffer, which she may refuse.

Agree_____　　　　　　　Disagree_____

Reasons:

3.　Arnold is offered a job in Silver's Gym, flexing his lats and pecs, and training flabby clients. One condition of the employment agreement is that if Arnold leaves Silver's, he cannot go to work for another fitness facility within the county for one year. This is an unenforceable covenant not to compete.

Agree_____　　　　　　　Disagree_____

Reasons:

4.　If Rockefeller Foundation promises to give the City Hospital $200,000 toward a new building project, this is a gift, and not a contract on which Hospital can reasonably rely, because it lacks a present, bargained for exchange.

Agree_____　　　　　　　Disagree_____

Reasons:

5.   When Arthur the Antique Dealer promised to deliver a Queen Anne chest to Diane, he had no idea that a tornado would come by and destroy his shop. Diane demands that he find another Queen Anne chest, exactly like the one she ordered. He can defend against the duty to deliver on the grounds of impracticability.

Agree_____   Disagree_____

Reasons:

CH. 11 - Sales and the UCC

OVERVIEW AND CHAPTER OUTLINE

This chapter provides a general introduction to the law of sales as set forth in Article 2 of the UCC and the law of negotiable instruments under Article 3. It considers the nature of sales contracts, the special requirements that the UCC places on merchants, and the performance obligations and warranty rights of parties to a sales contract. The chapter closes with a discussion of negotiable instruments and their relation to both the sale of goods and the law of contracts.

I.   **SCOPE OF SALES CONTRACTS UNDER THE UCC**

    A.   Relationship Between Article 2 and the Common Law

    B.   Sales, Goods, and Merchants Under the UCC

        1.   Sales

        2.   Goods

        3.   Merchants

II. **FORMING A SALES CONTRACT**

    A.   Intent to Contract

A.   Warranties of Title

B.   Express Warranties

C.   Implied Warranties

    1.   Implied Warranties of Merchantability

    2.   Implied Warranty of Fitness for a Particular Purpose

    3.   Implied Warranties Arising Under Trade Usage

D.   Warranty Disclaimers

E.   Third Party Beneficiaries of Warranties

    1.   Juris*prudence*? Does It Come with a Warranty?

IV.   RIGHTS AND REMEDIES

A.   Seller's Rights and Remedies

B.   Seller's Incidental Damages

C.   Buyer's Rights and Remedies

D.   Buyer's Incidental and Consequential Damages

    1.   Incidental Damages

    2.   Consequential Damages

V.   NEGOTIABLE INSTRUMENTS

A.   Origin of the Law of Negotiable Instruments

B.   The Functions of Negotiable Instruments

C.   Types of Negotiable Instruments

    1.   Orders to Pay: Drafts

    2.   Orders to Pay: Checks

VI. **SUMMARY**

VII. **ISSUE: HIGH TECH HELPS BUSINESS AND CRIMINALS?**

KEY WORDS AND PHRASES

Sales contracts	Warranty disclaimers
Sale of goods	Draft
Merchants	Drawer
Merchantability	Drawee
Sale	Payee
Gift	Time draft
Goods	Sight draft
Moveable goods	Trade acceptance agreement
Tangible goods	Sales draft
Good faith	Check
Output contract	Cashier's check
Requirements contract	Notes
Option contract	Maker
Firm offer	Payee
Good-faith dealing	Promissory notes
Trade usage	Collateral note
Perfect tender rule	Real estate mortgage
Cure	Installment note
Installment contract	Balloon note
Warranty	Certificate of deposit
Warranty of title	Assignment
Express warranty	Negotiation
Implied warranty	Bearer instruments

Negotiable (Nonnegotiable) Holder in due course
Order paper Ordinary holder
Bearer paper

FILL-INS

1._____ The UCC rule that looks to normal business practices to determine the existence of a contract when parties buy and sell goods using their own printed standard-order forms.

2._____ An acknowledgment from a bank that it has received money from a customer with a promise that the bank will repay the money at a specific date, or on demand.

3._____ An agreement among sixty-two nations of rules governing contracts for the sales of goods.

4._____ All things which are tangible and moveable at the time of identification to the contract for sale.

5._____ The court will fill in the gaps of sales contracts by looking to this, the regular practice and method of dealing in a specific trade.

6._____ The seller's right to repair or replace defective goods which the buyer has rightfully rejected.

7._____ Under Article 2, no new consideration is needed when this occurs as the parties perform their contract obligations.

8._____ An agreement by the buyer to purchase the seller's total output.

9._____ Honesty in fact in the conduct of the transaction incurred.

10._____ A transaction involving goods in which there is a "passing of title from the seller to the buyer for a price."

11._____ An offer in which some major terms were omitted or left for determination at some later time.

12._____   A seller or buyer who regularly deals in goods of the kind involved in the subject transaction.

13._____   A contract that provides for delivery in two or more separate lots.

14._____   A process of transferring an instrument so that the transferee takes the instrument free of any of the transferor's contract responsibilities, and may acquire better rights than the transferor had.

15._____   A transaction that is not a sale because no price is included.

16._____   The signed writing in which a merchant gives assurance that an offer will remain open for a stated time period.

17._____   A classification of commercial paper in which one party promises to pay a certain sum of money to another party.

18._____   A holder of a negotiable instrument against whom most defenses to the duty to pay made by the drawer or maker will not be allowed.

19._____   A seller's promise or guarantee as to the quality, safety, performance or title to goods being sold.

20._____   The performance obligations of this party are to accept and pay for the goods in accordance with the contract.

21._____   An unconditional written order to pay that involves three parties, in distinct capacities.

MULTIPLE CHOICE QUESTIONS

Select the best answer to each of the following questions.

1._____   General contract law, as distinguished from Article 2, Sales, governs which of the following contracts:

    a.   the sale of plastic molding.

    b.   the sale of an office building.

    c.   the sale of shares of stock.

    d.   all of the above.

    e.   only b and c of the above.

2._____   Under the UCC definition of "merchant," which of the following satisfy that definition?

    a.   An automotive dealer when selling a car.

    b.   A food broker when buying tomatoes.

    c.   A furniture manufacturer who sells bedroom suites through a retail outlet.

    d.   All of the above.

    e.   Only a and c of the above.

3._____   Which of the following is true?

    a.   A negotiable instrument can be transferred by assignment.

    b.   Where negotiable instruments are made payable "to the order" of a payee, endorsement and delivery are required for negotiation.

    c.   A draft made payable "to cash" requires no endorsement.

    d.   B and c only.

    e.   All of the above.

4._____   Article 2 modifies the common law of contracts in which of the following ways?

    a.   Intent to contract may be inferred from any reasonable response of the parties.

    b.   Acceptance need not contain terms that are exactly same as those in the offer.

    c.   The parties do not need new consideration to modify the terms of the contract if the reason is made in good faith.

    d.   The parties may decide to leave the price term open when they form the contract because of rapidly changing market conditions which might favor one or the other at the time of performance.

    e.   All of the above.

5._____   Which of the following is not true of transactions involving international sales of goods?

    a.   Former Communist countries have little experience with modern common law or UCC principles.

    b.   Japan, France, and Germany follow civil law but not common law principles.

    c.   The U.N. Convention on the International Sales of Goods follows common law principles more than civil law concepts.

    d.   The U.N. Convention allows enforcement of both written and oral contracts.

    e.   The U.N. Convention does not require consideration for the creation of a contract.

6._____   Which of the following is not a negotiable instrument?

    a.   Checks.

    b.   Trade acceptance agreements.

    c.   Installment contract.

    d.   Real estate mortgage.

    e.   Cashier's check.

7._____   If the seller delivers nonconforming goods:

    a.   the seller may cure if there is time remaining on the contract, and notifies the buyer of this intention.

    b.   the buyer may properly cancel the contract and sue for damages if the seller fails to cure.

    c.   the buyer may inspect the goods and withhold payment.

    d.   the buyer may revoke acceptance if the nonconformity substantially impairs the value of the goods.

    e.   all of the above.

8._____   Under the UCC, warranties:

    a.   are the seller's promise or guarantee that the goods are conforming to some specified standard.

    b.   must always be in writing to prove the seller's intent.

    c.   may be express or implied depending on who is selling the goods and what the nature of the representation is.

    d.   all of the above.

    e.   only a and c of the above.

9.____   When the seller decides to disclaim or limit a warranty,

      a.   the UCC allows great flexibility because the buyer should beware of the quality of the goods.

      b.   express warranties may not be disclaimed.

      c.   only time periods of warranties may be excluded.

      d.   buyers' remedies for breach may not be disclaimed.

      e.   none of the above are correct.

10.____   When an instrument is negotiable, which of the following characteristics must it possess?

      a.   be in writing and signed by the maker or drawer.

      b.   contain a sum certain.

      c.   must be payable on demand or at a specified time.

      d.   all of the above.

      e.   only a and b of the above.

MATCHING

Match the following terms or phrases to the descriptions below.

a.   Orange and Rockland Utilities, Inc. v. Amerada Hess Corporation

b.   Open price term

c.   Merchant's firm offer

d.   Gateway Company v. Charlotte Theaters

e.   Ramirez v. Autosport

f.   Incidental damages

g.   <u>Reid v. Eckerds Drugs</u>

h.   Order paper

i.   Negotiable instruments

j.   Implied warranty of merchantability

k.   Bearer paper

l.   Consequential damages

m.   Open delivery term

n.   AGBG

o.   UCC statute of frauds

p.   Installment contracts

q.   Express warranty

r.   Implied warranty of Fitness for a Particular Purpose

s.   Perfect tender rule

t.   Third party beneficiaries of warranties

1.____   Any sale of goods priced at $500 or more must be evidenced by a signed writing and contain a quantity term.

2.____   This may be made by any seller who has reason to know the buyer's specific purpose and on whose expertise the buyer actually relied.

3.____   The German Law on General Business Terms which is a commercial code much like the UCC.

4.____   A seller's confirmation or promise of fact, description of the goods, or sample or model of the goods may constitute this in the absence of intent.

5._____   These include costs resulting from a buyer's breach of contract, including expenses of stopping delivery and reselling goods.

6._____   Unless the parties have otherwise agreed, the goods must be delivered to the buyer at the seller's place of business, residence, or the location of the goods.

7._____   The court held that a failure to warn consumers of all dangerous tendencies of a product may breach the UCC's implied warranty of merchantability.

8._____   This instrument is payable to any party who presents it for collection.

9._____   A single contract that provides for delivery in two or more units.

10._____   The seller who makes this representation must be a merchant.

11._____   The court held in this case that a "requirements" clause in a contract need not be enforced when the complaining buyer failed to deal in good faith with the supplier in unforeseeable circumstances of rapidly rising fuel oil prices.

12._____   A negotiable instrument requiring both endorsement and delivery for negotiation.

13._____   The foreseeable damages to the buyer that may result from the seller's breach of contract.

14._____   This court held that a covering letter may be part of a total agreement as a modification.

15._____   A doctrine of common law origin that places an obligation on the seller to transfer and deliver conforming goods to the buyer.

16._____   A written promise or order to pay a certain sum of money that functions as a substitute for cash.

17._____   The court held that the seller's failure to cure minor defects will allow a buyer to rightfully reject the goods, cancel the contract, and demand recision.

18._____   A signed writing made by a merchant that an offer to sell or buy goods will be held open for a certain time.

19._____   The buyer's family and house guests.

20._____   The price which is commercially reasonable at the time and place of delivery.

CASE PROBLEMS

1.   Sammy Seller sent Christmas trees to Billy Buyer in the city, who had ordered eight dozen fir trees, between five and seven feet in height. When the trees arrived, Billy discovered that they were cedars, and that the shortest of them was eight feet. In fact, they were thin, not well filled out, and had many branches broken. Does he have any duty to Sammy under Article 2? What action(s) should he take?

_____

_____

_____

2.   When Lamon Brothers became PlastiTech and decided to revise their sales contracts to conform with the UCC, what terms did they need to include, and what terms could they omit?

_____

_____

_____

3.   Herman wrote to Matthew and suggested that they discuss Herman's purchase of certain machine dies that Matthew's company made. Herman intended to use the dies in his manufacturing plant. Herman signed the letter, and mailed it. When Matthew received the letter, he called Herman and discussed the terms of the deal over the telephone. Having reach an agreement, he jotted the number of dies, their dimensions, and the material from which they should be manufactured, initialed the notes, and sent the letter back to Herman. Later, after performance was begun, Matthew wanted to cancel the deal. Does Herman have enough of a writing sufficient to satisfy the Statute of Frauds?

_____

_____

_____

4. Bartram, Inc. contracted with Southwire to purchase a certain quantity of electrical connectors for use in a manufacturing project in which it was involved. After Southwire worked up the order and delivered, Bartram refused to accept the connectors on the grounds that its project had been canceled and thus it no longer had need of the goods. Is this a commercially sound reason under the UCC? What remedies does Southwire have, if any?

_____

_____

_____

5. On September 7, 1994, Annie, an accountant, was offered an opportunity to purchase a $2000 promissory note for $1650. The note was due and payable by Old Trusty Savings and Loan Bank on July 31, 1995, to someone whom Annie did not know, a fellow whose name on the note was Mack D. Nife. Suspicious, she asked Larry, the lawyer who made her the offer, if there was some problem with the note. He replied that there was nothing wrong with it, so far as he knew. He was merely trying to sell it for a client who was down on his luck and needed the money. What would you advise Annie to do?

_____

_____

_____

APPLICATION QUESTIONS

DO YOU AGREE OR DISAGREE WITH THE FOLLOWING STATEMENTS? JOT DOWN YOUR REASONS.

1.   Sally leaves her wedding pictures with the local drugstore photo development pickup station to be processed. A week later she pays for the pictures, but to her horror she discovers that they are murky and the negatives have been ruined by the processing lab. Does Sally have a breach of warranty claim against the drugstore?

Agree_____   Disagree _____

Reasons:

2.   The "Five and Dime" craft shop faxes its distributor of many years to order 14 dozen boxes of assorted Christmas decorations, "as usual." There is no mention of price or date of delivery. Could this possibly be construed to be a binding contract?

Agree _____   Disagree _____

Reasons:

3.   Juanita in Mexico wants to sell her turquoise and silver jewelry to a shop in Georgia. She has spoken with the Georgia buyer several times, and they have agreed on the quantity, price, and date of delivery. However, there is nothing in writing. Is this an enforceable contract?

Agree _____   Disagree _____

Reasons:

4.   Wood World offers to sell 24 of its fiberboard panels for $6 each to a local contractor, with the offer to remain open for the next 10 days. When the contractor fails to respond within that time, Wood World sells the boards to another contractor. Shortly afterwards, the first contractor appears to pick up the boards, and is furious to find that they are no longer available. Did Wood World make him a firm offer which he can enforce?

Agree _____   Disagree _____

Reasons:

5.   Hank owes Jerry $500, and gives him a letter stating, "I owe you $500, which I will pay to you or anyone you designate in 10 equal monthly installments, beginning today Nov. 1, 1993, at 7% interest per annum;" and signed the letter. Is this a negotiable promissory note?

Agree _____   Disagree _____

Reasons:

CH. 12 - Debtor / Creditor Relations

OVERVIEW AND CHAPTER OUTLINE

The chapter begins with an overview of debtor/creditor relations and then considers the law's impact on business as a creditor and the importance of credit and debt collection policies. The role of perfected security interests and mechanic's, possessory, and court-decreed liens in debt collection is then reviewed. The legal environment for a business as a debtor is considered next. The section then deals with the various rights and responsibilities accorded the creditor when a debtor is unable to meet its financial obligations. In particular, it considers the types of loans many businesses encounter in their operations and the legal protection for the creditors. The final sections provides an overview of federal bankruptcy law. It outlines the major provisions of the Bankruptcy Code, the role of the trustee in bankruptcy, and the priority of creditors.

I. **CREDITORS**

    A.   Credit Policy

        1.   Credit Accounts

        2.   International Perspectives: The Check is in the (Foreign) Mail

        3.   Collections Policy

    B.   Credit with Security

        1.   By Agreement

KEY WORDS AND PHRASES

Creditor

Debtor

Principal

Open account

Unsecured (or general) creditor

Insolvent

Secured creditor

Security (collateral)

Real property

Personal property

Mortgage

Secured transaction

Security interest

Attached

Perfected
Default
Priority
Lien
Garnishment
Mechanic's lien
Possessory (or artisan's) lien
Attachment lien
Writ of attachment
Judgment lien
Abstract of judgment
Writ of execution
Equity financing
Debt financing
Guaranty (or suretyship)
Surety
Performance
Guarantor

Exoneration
Subrogated
Nonexempt property
Homestead exemption
Tangible property
Floating lien
Statutory redemption period
Bankruptcy Reform Act
        (Bankruptcy Code) of 1978
Chapter 7
Involuntary bankruptcy
Liquidation
Bankruptcy discharge
Chapter 11
Reorganization
Debtor in possession
Composition

FILL-INS

1._____   Credit extended for sales of goods and services on the basis of an invoice, not a written contract.

2._____   The collateral offered by the debtor to the seller to secure credit.

3._____   Moveable property such as automobiles, furniture, and jewelry.

4._____   The agreement providing security for a credit transaction involving real estate.

5._____   The creditor's legal right in the product to secure payment of the sales price.

6._____   A security interest that has been attached with legal notice given, usually through filing.

7._____   The legal hold that a creditor organization has over the product of a customer to secure payment for that product.

8._____   A method organizations use to raise funds through sale of the corporation's stock.

9._____   This is a third party's guarantee or promise to pay the debt of an organization if the debtor does not pay.

10._____   The process by which a surety may seek reimbursement against the debtor organization.

11._____   A security interest in inventory which attaches to replacement stock.

12._____   The time within which the debtor organization may pay its debt and take back foreclosed property.

13._____   The federal statute that governs official bankruptcy procedure.

14._____   The individual appointed to administer the debtor's estate.

15._____   The order by which classes of creditors receive shares of the debtor's estate to pay for the debts owed them.

16._____   This provides debtors with an opportunity to restructure or reorganize their businesses in bankruptcy.

17._____   An agreement which debtor businesses may use in the U.S. to repay a percentage of their debts to creditors, outside of bankruptcy.

18._____   This allows more time for a debtor to pay his creditors.

19._____   This agreement between the debtor and all creditors assigns all nonexempt assets to a trustee who liquidates the assets and distributes the proceeds to the creditors on a percentage basis.

20._____   Article 9, UCC, established this process so that products may secure the extension of credit in the sales transaction.

MULTIPLE-CHOICE QUESTIONS

Select the best answer to each of the following questions.

1._____   Dun and Bradstreet is a business credit reporting company. Which of the following statements is <u>not</u> true?

        a.   D & B may solicit financial information from companies as to their creditworthiness.

        b.   D & B may use public data sources to determine creditworthiness.

        c.   D & B may not use business competitors as sources of financial data.

        d.   D & B may sell credit reports and credit ratings about companies it has investigated.

2._____   When a business organization establishes a credit policy for its customers, it may:

        a.   Consider the customer's character in honoring promises to pay.

        b.   Obtain past payment records and observations of management style.

        c.   Investigate the customer's collateral.

        d.   A, B, and C.

        e.   A and C only.

3._____   When a creditor organization tries to insure that it collects bills from its customers, it:

     a.   May allow some customers to be unsecured creditors and require security from other customers.

     b.   Must use Article 9, UCC, with personal property transactions.

     c.   Must attach real property through the process known as perfecting the security interest.

     d.   May not repossess consumer goods without giving notice to all other parties who may have interests in the goods.

4._____   When a creditor organization faces default by a customer/debtor, it:

     a.   May not repossess the secured property if this requires a breach of the peace.

     b.   May use a Mechanic's Lien without agreement by the debtor.

     c.   May possess or hold goods to which it has added value until the customer pays for them.

     d.   A and C.

     e.   A, B, and C.

5._____   When a creditor sues a debtor on past due bills, the court may:

     a.   Order the property to be seized to prevent the debtor from disposing of it.

     b.   Grant an abstract of judgment which the creditor may file.

     c.   Issue a writ of execution allowing the sheriff to seize and sell the property and distribute the proceeds to the creditor.

     d.   B and C

     e.   A, B and C

6.____   With regards to suretyship, which of the following statements is <u>false</u>?

    a.   A common form of suretyship is a co-signature on a bank loan.

    b.   Suretyship can be created by the oral agreement of the principal and the debtor.

    c.   Bankruptcy can never be a defense for a surety.

    d.   All of the above.

    e.   B and C only.

7.____   Which of the following is <u>not</u> necessary to perfect a security interest?

    a.   A security agreement.

    b.   A signed financing statement.

    c.   The debtor's financial statement.

    d.   Filing the financing statement.

    e.   Goods for sale.

8.____   When a business has debts greater than assets, which of the following alternatives are available?

    a.   It may file for Chapter 7 or 11.

    b.   It may file for Chapter 13.

    c.   It may exempt some property from bankruptcy.

    d.   All of the above.

    e.   A and C only.

9.____   When a U.S. organization is in financial distress it may avoid bankruptcy by all of the following <u>except</u>:

     a.   Reorganizing under the Composition Act.

     b.   Reaching a contractual agreement with its creditors for an extension of time.

     c.   Bargaining with its creditors to pay some percentage of the total due then.

     d.   Having a trustee sell its non-exempt assets and distribute the proceeds to all its creditors.

MATCHING

Match the following terms or phrases to the descriptions below.

a.   General creditor

b.   Secured creditor

c.   Open account

d.   <u>Dunn & Bradstreet v. Greenmoss Builders</u>

e.   Real property

f.   Attached security interest

g.   Attachment lien

h.   Default

i.   <u>Holly Lake Association v. FNMA</u>

j.   Writ of execution

k.   Exoneration

l.   <u>Travis Pruitt & Assoc. v. Smith</u>

m.   Homestead exemption

n.   Working capital loan

o.   <u>Pecora v. First Bank of Georgia</u>

p.   Mortgage

q.   Liquidation in bankruptcy

r.   Suretyship

s.   Discharge in bankruptcy

t.   <u>In the Matter of Gaslight Club, Inc.</u>

1._____   This case held that courts have broad discretion to appoint new trustees to replace the debtor in possession.

2._____   This creditor is unsecured against its debtor.

3._____   This Chapter 7 proceeding terminates the debtor's business.

4._____   This kind of credit arrangement defines the credit period and any discounts available to the debtor.

5._____   This provision allows a debtor to protect his "shelter" from creditors.

6._____   This case deals with a small business owner who failed to record deeds showing that a security deed existed encumbering property which was later used as collateral for a loan.

7._____   This creditor under Article 9 has attached and perfected a security interest in collateral used to secure debt.

8._____   This court order relieves the debtor of obligations to repay certain debts.

9._____   This case decision allowed punitive damages to be assessed against a false credit report.

10._____	This Article 9 interest is based on a security agreement and a signed financing statement.

11._____	This court considered which creditor had a prior lien.

12._____	This contract is a promise by a third party to be responsible for the debtor's repayment.

13._____	This case held this debtor personally liable as a surety for the debts of his company.

14._____	This property involving land is not subject to Article 9, UCC.

15._____	This occurs when a debtor fails to pay the creditor the money owed.

16._____	This line of credit provides cash to a business to purchase real property, inventory, and leases.

17._____	This is a court order requiring that the debtor organization perform/pay for the benefit of the surety.

18._____	This legal document is a lien against real estate giving the holder the right to sell the property if the debtor defaults.

19._____	This court order allows the sheriff to seize and sell property of the debtor.

20._____	This is a court order allowing seizure of goods to prevent disposition by a debtor in default.

CASE QUESTIONS

1.	George the Florist needs to keep a supply of floral products in his shop for sale to customers, but he does not have enough cash to pay for them until he can sell them. What can he do to purchase the inventory?

_____

_____

_____

2.   If George agrees to put up collateral for his credit, does this mean his transaction is an Article 9 secured transaction?

_____

_____

_____

3.   If George is approached by a customer who wants to purchase floral arrangements on credit, must George grant credit under Article 9?

_____

_____

_____

4.   If George's customers are slow to pay and the Florist shop comes into financial distress, should George file for bankruptcy?

_____

_____

_____

5.   If bankruptcy becomes necessary, what are George's options?

_____

_____

_____

APPLICATION QUESTIONS

Do you agree or disagree with the following statements? Jot down your reasons.

1.   Banks may repossess collateral if their records show the debtor to be in default.

Agree_____   Disagree_____

Reasons:

2.   Credit managers should use Article 9, secured transactions law in all cases where customers want to buy goods on credit.

Agree_____   Disagree_____

Reasons:

3.   Do you agree with the vice president for credit at Levi Strauss who complained that "Bankruptcy has become an acceptable strategy for resolving business problems"?

Agree_____   Disagree_____

Reasons:

4.   Creditors can ignore the bankruptcy proceedings filed by their debtors and thus escape the discharge orders.

Agree_____   Disagree_____

Reasons:

CH. 13 - Agency

OVERVIEW AND CHAPTER OUTLINE

This chapter provides an overview of agency law, beginning with a discussion of the nature and formation of the relationship, and the legal constraints on its functions. Agencies are compared to master-servant and independent contractor relationships. The chapter examines the agent's authority and the principal's liability in contracts and torts. The chapter concludes with termination of agency relationships. Agency relationships permit business to expand by allowing a principal to engage many agents and carry on business in several places at the same time. Agency is the foundation of corporation law and, thus, has contributed to the growth and expansion of business activities.

I.   **AGENCY RELATIONSHIP**

    A.   Creating an Agency

        1.   Agency by Agreement of the Parties

        2.   Agency by Ratification by the Principal

        3.   Agency by Estoppel

        4.   Agency by Operation of Law

B.　　Classification of Agents

1.　　Universal Agents

2.　　General Agents

3.　　Special Agents

4.　　Agency Coupled with an Interest

5.　　Gratuitous Agent

6.　　Subagents

II.　AGENTS COMPARED TO EMPLOYEES AND CONTRACTORS

A.　　Master-Servant Relationship

1.　　Employees as Servants and Agents

B.　　Employer-Independent Contractor Relationship

1.　　Juris*prudence*? Who, Him? Must Be An Independent Contractor

2.　　Contractors as Agents

3.　　Determining Liability

4.　　Juris*prudence*? My Tenants Are Doing What?

III.　DUTIES OF THE AGENCY PARTIES

A.　　Principal's Duties to an Agent

1.　　Duty to Cooperate with the Agent

2.　　Duty to Compensate the Agent

3.　　Duty to Reimburse the Agent's Reasonable Expenses

4.　　Duty to Indemnify the Agent for Losses

B.   The Agent's Liability

VII.   **TERMINATION OF AN AGENCY**

VIII. **SUMMARY**

XI.   **ISSUE: WHY ARE BUSINESSES HIRING INDEPENDENT CONTRACTORS?**

KEY WORDS AND PHRASES

Agency relationship	Fiduciary
Agent	Duty of loyalty
Principal	Confirmation plan
Power of attorney	Extension
Ratification	Bank workout
Express ratification	Assignment
Implied ratification	Assignee
Agency by estoppel	Trustee
Authority	Duty of obedience and performance
General agent	Reasonable care
Universal agent	Duty to account
Special agent	Actual authority
Agency coupled with an interest	Apparent authority
Gratuitous agent	Express authority
Subagents	Implied authority
Master - servant	Restatement of Agency (2d)
Employer - independent contractor	Disclosed principal
Servant (employee)	Partially disclosed principal
Master (employer)	Undisclosed principal
Independent contractor	Vicarious liability
Duty to cooperate	Respondeat superior
Duty to compensate	Termination
Duty to reimburse	Termination by operation of law
Duty to indemnify	

FILL-INS

1. _____   Occurs when the agent or principal dies.

2. _____   This relationship results from a principal's words or actions which may lead a person reasonably to believe that he or she has authority to act as an agent.

3. _____   Sometimes referred to as real authority because it is authority actually given by the principal to the agent.

4. _____   Duty to carry out responsibilities for a principal with the degree of care that a reasonable person would exercise under the circumstances.

5. _____   A classification of agents under which an individual is designated by an principal to do all acts that can be legally delegated to an agent.

6. _____   An agent's duty to account for the funds and property of the principal that have been entrusted to the agent or that comes into his/her possession.

7. _____   An affirmation by the principal of an unauthorized agreement entered into by an individual who is not an agent or an agent who is acting beyond his/her authority.

8. _____   A person who contracts with another to do something for him but who is not controlled by the other nor subject to the other's right to control with respect to his physical conduct in the performance of the undertaking.

9. _____   Individual who agrees to act on behalf of and for and to be subject to the control of another individual or company.

10. _____   Individuals appointed by an agent, intended to assist the agent in the performance of the agent's duties.

11. _____   Duty to pay for damages or, in effect, to insure the agent for losses suffered while undertaking authorized transactions on the principal's behalf.

12. _____   Includes the responsibility to pay the agent, to not wrongfully terminate the agency relationship, and, in some circumstances, to furnish the agent with a means of employment or opportunity to work.

13._____   Involves the principal's affirmative indication to either the individual or the third party to be bound to the otherwise unauthorized agreement.

14._____   A relationship in which an agent has paid for the right to exercise authority with regard to a business.

15._____   Authority that also arises in many cases when an agent receives express authority.

16._____   Means that the agent occupies a position of trust and confidence with regard to the principal.

17._____   In the absence of a formal agreement, under certain circumstances, an agency relationship imposed by the courts on the basis of public welfare.

18._____   Exists because the agent is required to meet a higher standard of conduct than that ordinarily imposed upon parties to business dealings.

19._____   Conduct or behavior on the part of the principal that is consistent with the existence of an agency relationship may be sufficient to bind the principal to contracts entered into thereby on the principal's behalf.

20._____   Describes the employment of an agent for the purpose of representation in establishing legal relations between a principal and third parties.

MULTIPLE CHOICE QUESTIONS

Select the best answer to each of the following questions.

1. _____   To hold a principal liable under the legal process of implied ratification, the:

    a.   Principal must have knowledge of the facts regarding the transaction taken on his/her behalf, yet remain silent.

    b.   Ratification must be in writing.

    c.   Agent must have been acting for a principal.

    d.   Agency must be established by necessity.

2. _____   An agency coupled with an interest will be created where:

   a.   An attorney is to receive 25% of a plaintiff's recovery for personal injuries.

   b.   A broker is to receive a 5% sales commission on the proceeds of a sale.

   c.   An employee is hired for a period of 3 years and is to receive $40,000 per year plus 2% of net sales.

   d.   A borrower pledges stock to a lender and authorizes the lender to sell the stock and apply the proceeds to the loan if the borrower defaults.

3. _____   Which of the following is not an essential element of an agency relationship?

   a.   It must be created by contract

   b.   Agent must be subject to principal's control

   c.   Agent is a fiduciary.

   d.   Agent acts on behalf of another.

4. _____   What fiduciary duty, if any, exists in an agency relationship?

   a.   There is no fiduciary duty in an agency relationship.

   b.   Agent owes fiduciary duty to principal.

   c.   Principal owes a fiduciary duty to the agent.

   d.   Agent owes a fiduciary duty to third parties with whom the agent deals with on behalf of the principal.

5. _____   Frank hires an agent to manage an apartment building. Later, without Frank's consent, the agent also becomes the manager of an apartment building across the street, owned by Adams. The agent has:

a.   Not breached any duty to Frank if managing Adams' building was not a full-time job.

b.   Not breached the agency relationship unless the agreement with Frank expressly excluded working elsewhere.

c.   Breached a duty to Frank.

d.   Not breached a duty if the agent can handle both jobs easily.

6. _____   Paul employed Terry as an agent to purchase a tract of real property. Terry is a:

a.   Universal agent.

b.   Servant.

c.   General agent.

d.   Special agent.

7. _____   Which of the following statements is not true?

a.   A servant is an employee who works under the direct control of the employer.

b.   A servant can never act on behalf of the employer in dealing with third parties.

c.   A servant can sometimes be an agent.

d.   An independent contractor is never an employee.

e.   An independent contractor is not subject to another's right of control with respect to the physical performance of the undertaking.

8. _____   Which of the following acts can a principal employ an agent to perform?

    a.   Sell real property.

    b.   Vote in a presidential primary.

    c.   Commit a crime.

    d.   Sign a will for the principal.

9. _____   A subagent:

    a.   Is an agent appointed by a principal to help an agent.

    b.   Has no fiduciary to the original principal.

    c.   Is an agent of an agent.

    d.   Does not have the power to subject the original principal to liability.

10. _____   An agency relationship:

    a.   Must be in writing.

    b.   Creates a fiduciary duty in the principal.

    c.   Can be created by estoppel.

    d.   Can never be terminated without the consent of both parties.

MATCHING

Match the following terms or phrases to the descriptions below.

a.   Implied ratification

b.   Right of Control

c.   Power of Attorney

d.   Duty to reimburse

e.   <u>Watson v. Schmidt</u>

f.   Independent contractors

g.   Civil law system of agency

h.   Agent's duty of obedience and performance

i.   General agent

j.   Special agent

k.   Duty to notify

l.   Master-Servant Relationship

m.   <u>Santiago v. Phoenix Newspapers, Inc.</u>

n.   Duty of complete and utmost loyalty

o.   Gratuitous agent

p.   <u>Tarnowski v. Resop</u>

q.   <u>Rosen v. DePorter-Butterworth Tours, Inc.</u>

r.   Express written authority

s.   Agency coupled with an interest

t.   Written agency contract

1. _____   This case held that a principal is entitled to recover from the agent any and all profits associated with contracts the agent enters into on the principal's behalf, even thought there is no actual injury.

2. _____   The agent's duty to keep the principal informed of all facts and occurrences relevant to the agency purpose.

3. _____   An individual who volunteers services to a principal without agreement or expectation of compensation.

4. _____   An agent authorized to execute all transactions connected with a particular business or trade.

5. _____   An agent's duty to follow, as closely as possible, all instructions provided by the principal.

6. _____   These parties, when hired, do not subject the employer to employment and insurance taxes, and most tort liability.

7. _____   A written agency contract which later proves to be invalid will not release a principal from liability to a third party.

8. _____   This case held that when a principal accepts in silence the benefits of a sale made by an agent who has acted without authority, the contract has been ratified.

9. _____   A written document authorizing an individual or company to act as an agent for a principal.

10. _____   Required where the agency relationship is to be for a period in excess of 1 year or is for the sale of land.

11. _____   Occurs when the principal behaves as if s/he has the intention of ratifying the unauthorized agreement.

12. _____   Principal's duty to pay reasonable expenses incurred by the agent in carrying out responsibilities under the agency.

13. _____   Describes the agency relationship where an agent has paid for the right to exercise authority with regard to a business.

14. _____   An agent with authority to execute a specific transaction or to undertake a specific act on behalf of the principal.

15. _____   An employment relationship whereby the employee is employed by the employer to perform some service or labor.

16. _____   This case held that in the event of a breach of contract, the agent is liable to third parties if the agent has not revealed the existence of the agency relationship or the identity of the principal.

17. _____   A legal document consisting of instructions given by the principal to an agent for the purpose of establishing broad or limited authority in the agent.

18. _____   Describes the duty that arises because the agent occupies a fiduciary relationship to the principal and is required to meet a higher standard of conduct than is ordinarily imposed upon parties to business dealings.

19. _____   This case held that an employer who controls duties, hours and method of work may be vicariously liable for the torts of an independent contractor.

20. _____   The single most important factor considered by a court in determining whether one is an employee or an independent contractor.

CASE PROBLEMS

1.   When the Alexanders applied for a mortgage loan, the bank president told them a termite inspection was always required and arranged for by the bank. Later, the bank president was advised that termites were found on the property and that extermination would be necessary, but he did not advise the Alexanders who subsequently purchased the property. Do the Alexanders have a cause of action against the bank?

_____

_____

_____

2.   Jane owes Paul $1,000, and the debt is due and payable. Jane does not have the cash to pay the debt, but she has a stereo worth $1,000. She gives it to Paul to sell to satisfy the debt, with any excess going to Jane. Later, Jane and Paul have a disagreement, and Jane sends a letter to Paul revoking the agency. Can she do it?

_____

_____

_____

3.   Black, a computer programmer, worked for Jurapple Park, a computer servicing agency, which provided temporary help services for area businesses. What must Jurapple show to avoid paying employment taxes on Black? What are the consequences to Black?

_____

_____

_____

4.   Johnson, an employee of Amax, Inc., became involved in an argument with Dixon, an employee of an independent contractor, LIC, performing painting work at the Amex plant. Dixon who was applying spray paint above Johnson's work area sprayed paint on Johnson. Johnson demanded that Dixon apologize. Dixon, who had been advised that his work had "top priority," refused. An argument took place and Dixon shoved Johnson against a steel beam. Johnson sued Dixon and LIC for injuries caused by the battery. LIC claims that it is not liable under the doctrine of respondeat superior because Dixon acted outside the scope of his employment. Is this correct?

_____

_____

_____

5.   The Rockefeller family wanted to give the United Nations a site on the East River to build a headquarters. The family knew that if the owners of the land knew who was buying the land and the reason for the purchases, they would raise prices dramatically. The family engaged a group of agents who were to purchase the land in their names, keeping the name of the true purchasers secret. If a breach of one of the sales contracts occurs, who can the seller sue?

_____

_____

_____

APPLICATION QUESTIONS

DO YOU AGREE OR DISAGREE WITH THE FOLLOWING STATEMENTS? JOT DOWN YOUR REASONS.

1. Annie Attorney allows Clyde Clerk to handle office interviews with her clients. If she does not fully explain the situation to the client, the client may reasonably believe that Clyde is the agent for Annie and can obligate her to the client.

   Agree_____   Disagree_____

   Reasons:

2. When Janet agrees to manage the Campus Snack Bar, she is paid weekly, given certain goals to fulfill, and given a degree of discretion in conducting the operations of the Snack Bar. This makes her an independent contractor.

   Agree_____   Disagree_____

   Reasons:

3. Ralph Route Man has the job of placing Kitty Cat food cans on shelves of the grocery stores on his route. When Kolin Competitor moves Kitty Cat cans so as to place his own in a more prominent position, Ralph punches him out. Kitty Cat is not vicariously liable for Ralph's tort because Kitty did not instruct Ralph to defend the shelf space by force of arms.

   Agree_____   Disagree_____

   Reasons:

4.   When Bobbie travels on University business, she can expect the employer to pay for her travel expenses and for her long distance telephone calls home to check on her own consulting business.

Agree_____   Disagree_____

Reasons:

5.   Tommy Tree Buyer sends Teddy Truck Driver onto the land of Teresa Third Party to cut and haul away some timber. Tommy knows that Teresa is unaware of this activity, and that by the time Teddy finishes, Teresa will not be able to prove that it was Tommy who took the trees. However, if Teresa sees Teddy in the act, and swears out a warrant against him for theft, Tommy will not be liable for the harm done either to Teresa or Teddy.

Agree_____   Disagree_____

Reasons:

CH. 14 - Business Organizations

OVERVIEW AND CHAPTER OUTLINE

This chapter discusses the various kinds of business organizations and the reasons for adopting one form over another. The various aspects of the sole proprietorship, partnership, and corporation are analyzed. It concludes with a discussion of alternative forms such as joint ventures, joint stock companies, cooperatives, syndicates, and private franchises.

I.   **SOLE PROPRIETORSHIPS**

II.   **PARTNERSHIPS**

      A.   International Perspectives: Small Is Not So Beautiful in Japan

      B.   Formation of a Partnership

            1.   Duty of Partners

            2.   Control of Partners

      C.   Termination of the Partnership

VI. **KEY ORGANIZATIONAL FEATURES**

    A.   Limited Liability

        1.   Entities with Unlimited Liability

        2.   Entities with Limited Liability

        3.   Juris*prudence*? And We Will Throw in the Brooklyn Bridge

    B.   Transferability of Ownership Interests

        1.   Nontraded Entities

        2.   Publicly Traded Corporations

    C.   Duration

        1.   Nontraded Entities

        2.   Corporations

VII. **OTHER BUSINESS ORGANIZATION FORMS**

    A.   Joint Ventures

        1.   International Perspectives: Avoiding Joint Venture Pitfalls in China

    B.   Joint Stock Companies

    C.   Cooperatives

    D.   Syndicates

VIII. **FRANCHISES**

    A.   Types of Franchises

    B.   The Law of Franchising

        1.   The FTC Franchise Rule

        2.   State Regulation

KEY WORDS AND PHRASES

Sole proprietorship
The owner is the business
General partnership
Uniform Partnership Act
Dissolution
New business
Winding up
Limited partnership
Partners
Uniform Limited Partnership Act
Revised Uniform Limited
    Partnership Act
Certificate of limited partnership
General partner
Limited partner
Corporation
Corporate charters
General incorporation statutes
Articles of incorporation
Certificate of incorporation
Legal entity
Bylaws
Shareholders
Stock certificate

Proxy
Resolutions
Board of directors
For cause
Breach of duty
Misconduct
Duty of care
Business judgment rule
Fiduciary duty of loyalty
Managers
Dissolution
Voluntary dissolution
Involuntary dissolution
Limited liability company (LLC)
Articles of organization
Members
Membership interest
Operating agreement
Transferability
Closed corporations
Duration
Perpetual existence
Joint venture
Joint stock company

Cooperative

Syndicate

Franchise

Franchisee

Franchisor

Federal Trade Commission's

    Franchise Rule

Franchise Agreement

FILL-INS

1. _____   A general partnership for a limited time and purpose.

2. _____   The name given to a group of individuals who join together to finance a specified project, such as a real estate development.

3. _____   Usually specifies such matters as the business name, relative ownership interests of the partners, and procedures for the partnership's dissolution.

4. _____   Early statutes establishing a simple procedure for incorporating a business.

5. _____   Is a business organization involving a unique mixture of partnership and corporation characteristics. Ownership is dictated by shares of stock, but it is created through an agreement.

6. _____   Occurs when an event takes place that precludes partners from engaging in any "new business."

7. _____   A special form of general partnership made up of two or more individuals who have entered into an agreement to carry on a business venture for profit. Not all partners have unlimited liability for the debts of the venture.

8. _____   A business organization made up of two or more individuals who have entered into an agreement, either express or implied, to carry on a business venture for profit.

9. _____   Requires that each partner act in good faith for the benefit of the partnership.

10. _____   Involves the actual process of completing any unfinished business of the partnership, collecting, and distributing the partnership's assets.

11._____   The "rules" that regulate and govern the internal operations of the corporation.

12._____   A business organization, which may or may not be incorporated, organized to provide an economic service to its members.

13._____   This business organization exists whenever a party is granted the right to sell goods or services according to the franchisor's marketing plan.

14._____   Are the owners of a corporation.

15._____   Are co-owners of a business and share control over the business's operations and profits.

16._____   Regulation by the Federal Trade Commission that is the primary federal regulation of franchises.

17._____   A change in the relationship of the partners demonstrating either an unwillingness or an inability to continue with the business of the partnership.

18._____   An individual conducting business for himself or herself.

19._____   This protects directors from honest mistakes in judgment not resulting from negligence.

20._____   This business organization is treated like a corporation for liability purposes but like a partnership for federal tax purposes.

MULTIPLE CHOICE QUESTIONS

Select the best answer to each of the following questions.

1. _____   For which of the following purposes is a partnership generally considered to be an entity?

   a.   Continuing existence.

   b.   Insulation of partners from personal liability.

   c.   Collect judgments in its own name.

   d.   Taxes.

2. _____   A certificate of limited partnership need not contain:

   a.   Name of the business.

   b.   Percentage of each limited partner's liability.

   c.   Type or character of the business.

   d.   Names and addresses of each general and limited partner.

3. _____   The general partnership and the corporation both:

   a.   Are treated for most purposes as entities distinct from their owners.

   b.   Are created at state law.

   c.   Are treated the same way for tax purposes.

   d.   Have perpetual existence.

4. _____   Which of the following is true about ending a partnership's existence?

    a.   The winding up process follows termination of the partnership's existence.

    b.   The winding up process involves cashing in and distributing partnership assets.

    c.   Dissolution follows termination of the partnership's existence.

    d.   Termination but not liquidation must follow dissolution.

5. _____   A limited partner:

    a.   Has no voting rights.

    b.   Is liable for obligations of the partnership to the extent of his/her capital contribution.

    c.   Has no right to look at partnership books.

    d.   Can participate in the day-to-day management of the partnership.

6. _____   As a general rule, a corporation can be formed by:

    a.   Approval of the Federal Trade Commission.

    b.   Simple agreement of investors.

    c.   Commencing to do business.

    d.   Issuance of a charter by a state.

7. _____   Wilson & Co. is a stock company. Which of the following is not true?

    a.   Ownership is represented by shares of stock.

    b.   It will be treated as a corporation for income tax purposes.

    c.   It is formed by agreement, not charter.

    d.   It may have perpetual existence.

8. _____ Which of the following statements is correct regarding a limited partnership:

    a. There must be at least three general partners.

    b. It can be created with limited liability for all partners.

    c. At least one general partner must be a limited partner.

    d. It can only be created pursuant to a statute providing for the formation of limited partnerships.

9. _____ Generally, articles of incorporation must contain all of the following except the:

    a. Name of the corporation.

    b. Name of the incorporators.

    c. Number of shares authorized.

    d. Names of initial officers and their terms of office.

10. _____ Partners occupy a fiduciary relationship toward each other. Because of this, partners:

    a. Must place their individual interests above those of the partnership.

    b. May engage in a business that competes with the partnership as long as partnership funds are not used.

    c. Must participate in the day-to-bay management of the partnership.

    d. May not earn a secret profit in dealings with the partnership or partners.

MATCHING

Match the following terms or phrases to the descriptions below.

a.   Shlensky v. Wrigley

b.   Dissolution

c.   Northampton Valley Constructors v. Horne-Lang Associates

d.   Tigrett v. Pointer

e.   Fiduciary duty of good faith

f.   Latta v. Kilbourn

g.   Limited partners

h.   Certificate of incorporation

I.   Articles of incorporation

j.   Fiduciary duty of loyalty

k.   Stock certificate

l.   Estate of Witlin

m.   Corporation

n.   Quorum

o.   Termination of the corporation

p.   Shareholders

q.   Day-to-day management of the corporation

r.   Resolutions

s.   Board of Directors

t.   Termination of the partnership

1. _____   This case held that limited partners are liable to creditors of the limited partnership only up to the amount of their required contributions and not up to the requirements of the limited partnership.

2. _____   This case held that partners must place their individual interests below those of the partnership.

3. _____   Are investors who do not (and may not) participate in the management of the business, and are not liable for the debts or torts of the business beyond their capital contributions.

4. _____   Along with an application, they must be filed with an appropriate officer of a state and generally provide the name and address of the corporation and the classes of stock to be issued and their par value.

5. _____   This is the form in which the corporate business is presented to the shareholders at a shareholders meeting and which they either approve or disapprove.

6. _____   Their obligations to the corporation's creditors are limited to the capital contribution made or expected to be made by them.

7. _____   Their functions include making basic corporate policy, including the sale of corporate assets and entrance into new corporate lines of business.

8. _____   This requires that directors place the interests of the corporation before their own interests.

9. _____   Like the termination of a partnership, it is essentially conducted in two phases, the dissolution phase and the winding up phase.

10._____   Is the form of business organization most often associated with the term business.

11._____   Occurs upon the happening of any event making the business of the partnership unlawful -- such as a legislative enactment.

12._____   This case held that the directors of the Cubs were not liable for negligence under the business judgment rule defense for failing to install lights at the field.

13._____   Is issued by the state after reviewing a corporation's articles of incorporation and its application.

14._____   It issued by a corporation to a stockholder and evidences an ownership interest in the corporation.

15._____   This case held that partners are under a fiduciary duty of loyalty to all partners involved in the business venture.

16._____   The duty of partners which forbids taking partnership assets and opportunities for oneself.

17._____   Is the responsibility of the board of directors which is delegated to hired managers.

18._____   This case held that when a corporation transfers virtually all of its assets to its controlling stockholder to repay its advances, without providing for other creditors, a court could determine whether his manipulation of the corporate form of business organization to serve his individual interests justifies imposition of personal liability.

19._____   Usually the more than fifty percent of the total shares held that must be represented at the shareholders' meeting.

20._____   A corporate decision requiring more than a simple majority as an action not within the ordinary course of the corporation's business.

CASE PROBLEMS

1.   Mike Middle Manager was given an early retirement from his company, and now he is anxious to start up a business which he can run himself. He reads the Wall Street Journal daily and is interested in buying one of the franchises that he sees advertised. Should he consult a lawyer before he buys the franchise?

_____

_____

_____

2. Johnson owned a piece of property. She asked her attorney, Adams, to have the property sold for $45,000. Adams was directed to have the property fully renovated. He was to be reimbursed for the renovation expenses and was to retain any profit from the sale over $45,000. Adams and Smith, a building contractor, agreed that Smith would do the renovating, receiving half the expenses and half of the profits Adams was to make on the sale. What is the relationship between Adams and Smith?

_____

_____

_____

3. Roy was a limited partner in the firm of Sobom. Roy took no personal part in the management of the business. Roy's son, Mark, was employed as the firm's bookkeeper. No note, check, or obligation could be signed by Sobom without the knowledge and approval of the bookkeeper. In a suit against the partnership, can Roy be held liable as a general partner?

_____

_____

_____

4. Anderson and Lawler intend to open a retail ice cream business. The store will be open for ninety hours a week. Anderson agrees to work fifty hours a week. Lawler will work forty hours. They agree to split the profits evenly, except that Anderson is guaranteed at least $10,000 of the profits, or the full amount if the business earns less than $10,000. Are Anderson and Lawler partners?

_____

_____

_____

5.   A stockholder learned that the corporation had paid over $1,000,000 in kickbacks and bribes. The board of directors admitted the allegations but said that the business judgment doctrine is a complete defense to this type of corporate activity. Is the board correct?

_____

_____

_____

APPLICATION QUESTIONS

DO YOU AGREE OR DISAGREE WITH THE FOLLOWING STATEMENTS? JOT DOWN YOUR REASONS.

1.   Albert and Burt agree to A & B's VCR repair shop with equal cash and work time contributions. They buy tools from C & D Supply, and begin business. When their store is robbed of all clients' VCRs while they have no insurance, they have to pay out all their company assets. Will Albert have to pay all of the money owed C & D's customers and suppliers out of personal funds when Burt declares bankruptcy?

Agree ____   Disagree ____

Reasons:

2.   If Ben goes to Jerry Attorney to pay him to file a corporate charter application for his new business, is the business protected by state corporate law before final issuance of the state corporate charter?

Agree ___   Disagree ____

Reasons:

3.   Ilene wants to raise money for a fabric and decorator supply store, but needs Ellen's money for start up capital. She prefers a joint venture form but Ellen wants to have a limited partnership. Does Ellen's preference provide Ilene with any limitations of liability?

        Agree _____   Disagree _____

        Reasons:

4.   If Ken wants to do business with Vasil to develop a fast food chain in the Czech Republic, will U. S. corporate law give Ken any protection in Prague?

        Agree _____   Disagree _____

        Reasons:

5.   Clyde has developed a chain of stores specializing in fried potato skins, called "Buffalo Chips." Can he sell this name to Marvin who wants to buy one of the stores as a franchisee?

        Agree ___   Disagree _____

        Reasons:

CH. 15 - Labor and Employment Law

OVERVIEW AND CHAPTER OUTLINE

This chapter details the major labor laws that have been enacted in the United States: Norris-LaGuardia Act, Wagner Act, Taft Hartley Act, and the Landrum-Griffin Act. The chapter discusses the processes and procedures used by the National Labor Relations Board and examines lawful and unlawful union activities. It concludes with an examination of nonunion employment laws affecting the labor relationship, including employment-at-will, worker health and safety, and occupational regulation.

I. **NATIONAL LABOR RELATIONS ACT**

    A.   Norris-LaGuardia Act

        1.   Injunctions Prohibited

    B.   Wagner Act of 1935

    C.   The Taft-Hartley Act of 1947

    D.   The Landrum-Griffin Act of 1959

        1.   Monitoring Leadership

        2.   Union Member Bill of Rights

II. **THE NATIONAL LABOR RELATIONS BOARD**

    A.   Unfair labor practice complaints

      1.   Inspections

      2.   Employee Rights

      3.   Penalties

  B.   Workers and Toxic Substances

      1.   Risks and Benefits

      2.   Hazard Communication Standard

VIII. WORKER'S COMPENSATION

  A.   Compensation Claims

  B.   Benefits and Incentives

      1.   Premiums Tied to Safety

      2.   A Flawed System?

      3.   Juris*prudence*? Watch Out for the Glazed Ones!

IX. GENERAL REGULATION OF LABOR MARKETS

  A.   Restrictions on Immigration

  B.   Federal Minimum Wage Requirements

  C.   Occupational Licensure and Regulation

      1.   Regulation Set by State Law

      2.   Juris*prudence*? You Want Me To Feed Him Too???

  D.   Warning Employees of Plant Closings

  E.   Family and Medical Leave

      1.   International Perspectives: Laws in Europe Restrict Employment at Will

  F.   Employee Retirement Plans

KEY WORDS AND PHRASES

National Labor Relations Act

Norris-LaGuardia Act

Labor disputes

Striking

Yellow-dog contracts

Wagner Act

National Labor Relations Board

Unfair Labor Practices

Taft-Hartley Act

Featherbedding

Landrum-Griffin Act

Representation election

Bargaining unit

Union certification

Exclusive bargaining agent

Decertification elections

Right-to-work laws

Closed shops

Union shops

Agency shops

Agency fees

Collective bargaining

Good faith bargaining

Mandatory subjects of bargaining

Grievance arbitration

Concerted activities

Primary boycott

Secondary boycott

Lockouts

Crossovers

Employment-at-will

Public policy exceptions

Wrongful discharge

Retaliatory discharge

Employment contract

Express contract

Implied contract

Implied covenant of good
    faith and fair dealing

Employee handbooks or manuals

Drug-Free Workplace Act

Occupational Safety and Health Act

Hazard communication standard

Workers' compensation laws

Immigration Reform and Control Act

Licensing requirements

Family and Medical Leave Act

Employee Retirement Income Security Act

Vesting

Worker Adjustment and
    Retraining Notification Act

FILL-INS

1._____ Provides that the expression of any views, arguments, or opinions or the dissemination thereof, whether in written, printed, graphic, or visual form, shall not constitute or be evidence of an unfair labor practice under any of the provisions of this Act, if such expression contains no threat of reprisal or force or promise of benefit.

2._____ Occurs when an employer attempts to bring economic pressure on a union by refusing to permit employees to work until the dispute is settled.

3._____ Usually is established to determine what the entry criteria will be for one to be licensed to practice an occupation.

4._____ This can create a binding contractual obligation if one can show the elements of offer, acceptance, and consideration in the employment process.

5._____ Its basic goal was to provide employees with the right to "self-organization to form, join, or assist labor organizations to bargain collectively through representatives of their own choosing, and to engage in other concerted activities for the purpose of collective bargaining or other mutual aid or protection."

6._____ Statutes requiring employers to pay employees or their heirs a benefit that is set by a compensation statute.

7._____ Created a bill of rights for union members.

8._____ Refers to the process by which the employer and the union negotiate a contract, setting forth the terms and conditions of employment for a given period of time.

9._____ Is a clearly legal strike by a union against the employer whose collective bargaining agreement is in question.

10._____ Initiated as a part of the Fair Labor Standards Act, these establish the lowest level of compensation as about 50 percent of average manufacturing wage.

11._____   Activities by two or more employees engaged in collective bargaining, strikes, or protests about unsafe working conditions.

12._____   Prohibit agency shops. Even if a majority of employees vote for union representation, no employee can be required to pay union fees.

13._____   Is a government agency whose primary responsibility is to conduct research related to occupational safety and health.

14._____   Allows employees to quit a job at any time for any reason and permits employers to dismiss employees without cause.

15._____   Are actions that would impair the basic goal of the NLRA, including employer interference with employee rights and employer formed or dominated "company unions."

16._____   Occurs when one tries to convince or force others to stop doing business with another company not directly involved in the primary labor dispute.

17._____   An employee who is aware of an illegal act at the place of employment and brings the act to the attention of the proper authorities.

18._____   A controversial emerging area of labor law for employers, who must prevent substance abuse in their businesses while minimizing the possibility of litigation problems caused by their invasion of employees' privacy rights.

19._____   An obligation to meet and be willing to present proposals and articulate supporting reasons, to listen to and consider the proposals of the other party, and to search for some common ground that can serve as the basis for an agreement but with no requirements of an agreement.

20._____   Under these clauses, disputes regarding a collective bargaining agreement, settled on by the employer and the union, are to be resolved by an internal grievance procedure.

MULTIPLE-CHOICE QUESTIONS

Select the best answer to each of the following questions.

1._____   Lockouts:

    a.   Are always illegal.

    b.   Are usually defensive, done in response to a strike, or to prevent a sit-down strike.

    c.   Will be upheld as long as they are used only to break the union or punish the workers.

    d.   Are strikes or other concerted action by a union against an employer of the employees whose collective bargaining agreement is in question.

2._____   This Act declared that public policy of the United States to be that the individual worker should have full freedom of association, self-organization, and designation of representatives of his own choosing, to negotiate terms and conditions of his employment.

    a.   Clayton Act.

    b.   Wagner Act of 1935.

    c.   Taft-Hartley Act of 1947.

    d.   Norris-LaGuardia Act.

3._____   Union representation elections:

    a.   Are called for by the NLRB when the union has collected valid cards from 25% or more of the employees.

    b.   Have been won by the unions slightly more than half the time they are held.

    c.   Determine whether a majority of employees want a particular union as their bargaining agent.

    d.   Are seldom held at the workplace.

4._____   Secondary boycotts:

    a.   Are legal strikes or other concerted actions by a union against the employer of the employees whose collective bargaining agreement in question.

    b.   Are illegal where the primary employer enters into an agreement with another firm to take partly completed goods and finish them for marketing.

    c.   Are illegal where an agreement is entered into between a union and its employer prohibiting the employer from dealing with certain other firms that could lead to a loss of jobs of employees at the unionized firm.

    d.   Occur when a union tries to convince or force others to stop doing business with another employer not directly involved in the primary labor dispute.

5._____   The Occupational Safety and Health Act of 1970 (OSHA) requires all of the following except:

    a.   Created the Occupation Safety and Health Commission, an agency responsible for implementing the OSHA.

    b.   Requires employers to keep records of work-related injuries, illnesses, and deaths, and to keep the workplace safe.

    c.   Requires that the responsible agency implement and enforce toxic substance standards for worker exposures.

    d.   Requires that a cost-benefit analysis be required as a justification for an OSHA standard.

6._____   Right-to-work Laws:

a.   Are in effect in several states, primarily in the northeast.

b.   Permit closed shops.

c.   Prohibit agency shops.

d.   Require that if a majority of employees vote for union representation and pay union initiation fees and dues, all employees can be required to pay agency fees.

7._____   The employment-at-will doctrine:

a.   Prohibits the firing of an employee who files a claim for workers' compensation.

b.   Permits the firing of an employee who voiced opinions to superiors about safety problems with a new product.

c.   Says that employers are not free to discharge employees for any reason at any time, and that employees are not free to quit their jobs for any reason at any time.

d.   Is primarily concerned with managerial and supervisory personnel.

e.   None of the above are correct.

8._____   The National Labor Relations Board (NLRB):

a.   Was created by the Taft-Hartley act.

b.   Opposes the introduction of grievance and arbitration procedures in labor contracts.

c.   Has statutory jurisdiction over all employers engaged in interstate commerce.

d.   Makes the final decision in a labor dispute brought to it.

9._____   Concerted activities:

    a.   Are prohibited where employers seek to use economic pressure to bear on employees but does permit employees to use such pressure.

    b.   Involve any joint actions by employees, such as a refusal to work on a certain job because of serious workplace hazards.

    c.   Permits employers to fire employees who leave the workplace without permission to protest conditions in the workplace.

    d.   Prohibits the firing of a worker who simply attacks a company in public without tying the attack to a union issue.

10._____   ERISA:

    a.   Has as its main objective preventing significant health risks in the workplace.

    b.   Is similar to Social Security in that it is primarily concerned with retirement plans for public employees.

    c.   Has as its main objective guaranteeing the expectations of retirement plan participants.

    d.   Requires that employee benefit plans must completely vest after five years of employment.

MATCHING

Match the following terms or phrases to the descriptions below.

a.   Metcalf v. Intermountain Gas Co.

b.   Jacksonville Bulk Terminal case

c.   Taft-Hartley Act

d.   Lechmere v. NLRB

e.   NLRB v. Katz

f.   Immigration Reform and Control Act

g.   Transworld Airlines v. Independent Federation of Flight Attendants

h.   Whirlpool Corp. v. Marshall

i.   Omnibus Transportation Employee Testing Act

j.   Employment Income Security Act (ERISA)

k.   Norris-LaGuardia Act

l.   Wagner Act

m.   Landrum-Griffin Act

n.   Chicago Teachers Union case

o.   Mandatory subjects of bargaining

p.   Geary v. U.S. Steel

q.   Workers' Compensation Laws

r.   Occupational Safety and Health Act

s.   American Textile Manufacturers v. Donovan

t.   Sheet Metal Workers v. Lynn

1.____   Prohibits federal courts from issuing injunctions in nonviolent labor disputes.

2.____   An Act of Congress requiring that all employers obtain and file proof of identity and U.S. citizenship or work authorization papers from all employees.

3.____   This case held that non-union employees could be charged an agency fee by a union to cover only the costs of collective bargaining representation.

4.____   This case held that an employee handbook could imply in good faith that employee sick leave was part of the contract.

5._____   This case held that an employer cannot unilaterally change the terms of an existing agreement with a union.

6._____   "Wages, hours, and other terms and conditions of employment" about which employers and unions must bargain in good faith but about which either party may insist on its position and back that insistence with a strike or a lockout.

7._____   Made the financial status of unions subject to federal review.

8._____   The court held that an employer is not required to lay-off junior cross-over employees or newly hired employees in order to bring back more senior employees who went on strike.

9._____   This case upheld the right of a company to fire a loyal employee who complained about an unsafe product, on the grounds that the company had a legitimate interest in preserving its normal operating procedures from the disruptions by its employees regardless of the employee's motivations.

10._____   "This remedy shall be exclusive in place of any and all other liability to such employees...entitled to damages in any action at law or otherwise on account of any injury or death...."

11._____   This case held that the Secretary of Labor could adopt a rule prohibiting employers from discriminating against employees who refused to work in unsafe working conditions.

12._____   Declared the public policy of the United States to be that the individual worker should "have full freedom of association, self-organization, and designation of representatives of his own choosing, to negotiate terms and conditions of his employment."

13._____   This case held that a union may not retaliate against a union member for speaking out against union policy and proposals.

14._____   This case held that cost benefit analysis is not required as a justification for an OSHA standard, noting that Congress "chose to place pre-eminent value on assuring employees a safe and healthful working environment, limited only by the feasibility of achieving such an environment."

15._____   This case held that the decision of the ILA to refuse to load ships bound for the Soviet Union as a protest to that country's invasion of Afghanistan constitutes a legitimate labor dispute under the Norris-La Guardia Act and not a political dispute.

16._____   Provides that employees "shall comply with occupational safety and health standards and all rules, regulations, and orders" that apply to them.

17._____   This act requires employers who operate transportation systems to test their employees for drug use.

18._____   This case upheld an employer's no-solicitation rule that was applied to all solicitations on company property.

19._____   Has as its main objective the guarantee of expectations of retirement plan participants.

20._____   Marked a change in federal policy from that of actively encouraging labor union formation to one of a generally favorable attitude toward unionization coupled with regulation.

CASE PROBLEMS

1.   Gateway Coal Co. signed a contract with a mine workers union that included 70% of the employees. Should the other 30% be able to avoid paying union dues and at the same time be able to benefit from collective bargaining activity?

_____

_____

_____

2.   Capital Times Company, a party to a government contract, posted a notice of its compliance with the Drug Free Workplace Act. When an employee came to work obviously "impaired," drove the company fork life off the loading dock, and injured himself badly, the personnel manager wanted to fire him. However, he did not want the liability that might arise from a lawsuit. What should he do? Explain.

_____

_____

_____

3. Bobby worked on board a barge in the Gulf of Mexico, and knew the Environmental Protection Agency had sent notice of a ban on the dumping of bilge water along the beaches. However, a long-standing practice in the barge trade was to dump bilge water whenever and where ever needed. When Bobby's captain told him to start the pumps, he objected. The captain fired him for insubordination. Does he have any legal claim against the captain? Explain.

_____

_____

_____

4. Pete's Printers uses a number of different kinds of chemicals and ink to stamp labels on plastic bags for several grocery chains. A clerical worker, not an employee who worked in the processing facility, but who worked in the "front office," complained of the fumes which she said made her throat swell up while she was at work. No one else complained of this symptom, and Pete was tired of hearing her. He told her to be quiet or be gone. She took him at his word and went directly to the OSHA office to see if they could help her. When she returned to Pete's, he told her she no longer was employed there. What rights does she have? What rights does Pete have?

_____

_____

_____

5. Dennis was working for his employer, Intertech, when an employee of another company came on to Intertech's property to make a delivery. Dennis attempted to receive the package, but the delivery person thought that Dennis was trying to take it without authority to do so. A scuffle followed, and Dennis was injured. Who will pay for Dennis' medical bills? Why?

_____

_____

_____

APPLICATION QUESTIONS

Marshall v. Barlow's, Inc.

U.S. Supreme Court
436 U.S. 307, 98 S. Ct. 1816 (1978)

Facts and Background. In 1975, an OSHA inspector entered Barlow's, Inc., a plumbing installation business. After showing his credentials, he informed Barlow officials that he wished to conduct a search of the working areas of the business.

Upon learning that there had been no complaint filed against Barlow's, that the search was simply the result of a random selection process, and that the inspector had no search warrant, Barlow to permit the inspection. Barlow relied on the Fourth Amendment's freedom from unreasonable searches and seizures.

Justice White delivered the opinion of the court.

***

The Warrant Clause of the Fourth Amendment protects commercial buildings as well as private homes. To hold otherwise would belie the origin of that amendment and the American colonial experience. An important forerunner of the first ten amendments to the United States Constitution, the Virginia Bill of Rights, specifically opposed "general warrants, whereby an officer or messenger may be commanded to search suspected places without evidence of a fact committed." The general warrant was a recurring point of contention in the colonies immediately preceding the Revolution.

***

The Secretary urges that an exception from the search warrant requirement has been recognized for "pervasively regulated business[es]."

***

Invoking the Walsh-Healey Act of 1936, the Secretary attempts to support a conclusion that all businesses involved in interstate commerce have long been subjected to close supervision of employee safety and health conditions. But the degree of federal involvement in employee working circumstances has never been of the order of specificity and pervasiveness that OSHA mandates. It is quite unconvincing to argue that the imposition of minimum wages and maximum hours on employers who contracted with the government under the Walsh-Healey Act prepared the entirety of American interstate commerce for regulation of working conditions to the minutest detail. Nor can any but the most fictional sense of voluntary consent of later searches be found in the single fact that one conducts a business affecting interstate commerce, under current practice and law, few businesses can be conducted without having some effect on interstate commerce.

***

We conclude that the concerns expressed by the Secretary do not suffice to justify warrantless inspections under OSHA or violate the general constitutional requirement that for a search to be reasonable a warrant must be obtained.

YOUR OPINION

1.   The Fourth Amendment was enacted to protect individuals in their homes. Does it also extend to businesses?

_____

_____

_____

2.   What fiction did the government rely on to justify the OSHA rule?

_____

_____

_____

3.   What are general warrants?

_____

_____

_____

4.   What did the Virginia Bill of Rights say about general warrants?

_____

_____

_____

5.   What is the holding of this case?

_____

_____

_____

CH. 16 - Employment Discrimination

OVERVIEW AND CHAPTER OUTLINE

This chapter traces the history of congressional efforts to define and control discrimination in employment. While the chapter focuses on the primary piece of legislation dealing with employment discrimination, Title VII of the Civil Rights Act of 1964, it also deals with age discrimination and with laws protecting persons who are disabled.

I.   **ORIGINS OF DISCRIMINATION LAW**

    A.   The Civil Rights Movement

    B.   Equal Pay Act of 1963

        1.   Enforcement Provisions

II.   **TITLE VII OF THE 1964 CIVIL RIGHTS ACT**

    A.   Protected Classes

        1.   Race

        2.   Color

        3.   National Origin

        4.   Religion

KEY WORDS AND PHRASES

The Equal Pay Act of 1963

Title VII of the Civil Rights Act of 1964

Equal Employment Opportunity
    Act of 1972

Equal Employment
    Opportunity Commission (EEOC)

Pregnancy Discrimination Act of 1978

Civil Rights Act of 1991

Discrimination

Race, color, religion,
    sex, or national origin

Equal employment opportunity

Protected classes

Reverse discrimination

Affirmative action programs

National origin

Undue hardship

Sexual harassment

Quid pro quo

Age Discrimination in
    Employment Act (ADEA)

Differential standards

Compensation differentials
Segregation
Harassment
Constructive discharge
Disparate treatment
Disparate impact
Intentional discrimination
Prima facie discrimination
Unintentional discrimination
Business necessity
Job related
Bona fide seniority or merit systems
Bona fide occupational qualification
Older Workers Benefit Protection
   Act (OWBPA)
Executive orders

Government contractors
Affirmative action
Work force analysis
Underutilization analysis
Rehabilitation Act
Americans with Disabilities
   Act of 1990 (ADA)
Person with disabilities
Substantial limitation of a
   major life activity
Reasonable accommodations
Undue hardship
ADA Enforcement Guidance:
   Preemployment Disability-Related
   Questions and Medical Examinations
   (1995)

FILL-INS

1._____   Promotes the employment of older individuals on the basis of their abilities rather than on their age.

2._____   Means to make a difference in treatment or [to] favor on a basis other than merit or ability.

3._____   This requires that each job be identified and then analyzed according to rank, salary, and the percentage of those employed in the job who come from each protected class.

4._____   The Act declares that Title VII's prohibitions on sex discrimination includes pregnancy, childbirth, and related medical conditions.

5._____   The President issued this to require government contractors to take affirmative action to remedy discriminatory practices.

6._____   Specific categories or classes of people which Congress sought to protect under Title VII.

7._____   Working conditions in which harassment is intolerable, causing the employee to quit.

8._____   Any person who has a physical or mental impairment which substantially limits one or more of a person's major life activities, has a record of such impairment, or is regarded as having such an impairment.

9._____   Compares the percentage of each protected class available in the community in each job category with that percentage actually employed by the contractor.

10._____   It was the first federal law that specifically addressed equal employment.

11._____   Provides for equal employment opportunity without regard for race, color, religion, sex, or national origin.

12._____   Is a conscious effort on the part of an employer to remedy discriminatory practices in the hiring, training, and promotion of protected class members to the extent a particular class (or classes) is under represented in the employer's workforce.

13._____   A job requirement that is necessary to the normal operation of the business, even if discrimination is permitted.

14._____   The employer must demonstrate this to defend or justify rules that have a discriminatory impact on employees.

15._____   Employees can rely on this theory if race, color, religion, sex, or national origin is involved in an employer's decision to hire, promote, or fire.

16._____   Prohibits public places from discriminating against individuals who have mental or physical disabilities.

17._____   Doctrine permits employers to set standards for employees regarding personal characteristics such as race or sex, but requires that the standards be applied equally.

18._____   This agency defined sexual harassment as "explicit or implicit promise of career advancement in return for sexual favors" (e.g., promotion, training, awards, details, lax timekeeping, and lower standards of performance).

19._____   Under this theory, an employer's neutral employment rule brings about discrimination.

20._____   Preferential treatment to members of protected classes.

MULTIPLE CHOICE QUESTIONS

Select the best answer to each of the following questions.

1._____   The Equal Pay Act of 1963:

    a.   Applies only to nonunion women employees.

    b.   Adopts the comparable worth principles of equal pay for comparable worth.

    c.   Is an amendment to the Civil Rights Act of 1871.

    d.   Does not apply to pay differentials based on seniority, merit, quality or quantity of production.

2._____   The Age Discrimination in Employment Act of 1967:

    a.   Does not apply to government agencies.

    b.   Applies to individuals between 20-30.

    c.   Is limited to hiring and promoting employees.

    d.   Applies generally to all employers that engage in interstate commerce and have 20 or more employees.

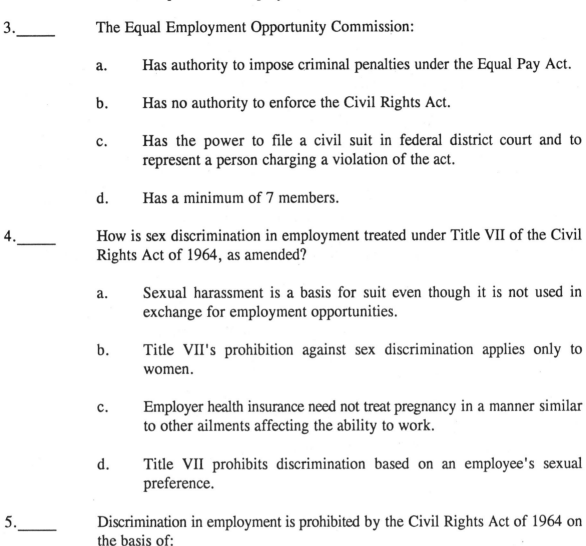

3.____   The Equal Employment Opportunity Commission:

    a.   Has authority to impose criminal penalties under the Equal Pay Act.

    b.   Has no authority to enforce the Civil Rights Act.

    c.   Has the power to file a civil suit in federal district court and to represent a person charging a violation of the act.

    d.   Has a minimum of 7 members.

4.____   How is sex discrimination in employment treated under Title VII of the Civil Rights Act of 1964, as amended?

    a.   Sexual harassment is a basis for suit even though it is not used in exchange for employment opportunities.

    b.   Title VII's prohibition against sex discrimination applies only to women.

    c.   Employer health insurance need not treat pregnancy in a manner similar to other ailments affecting the ability to work.

    d.   Title VII prohibits discrimination based on an employee's sexual preference.

5.____   Discrimination in employment is prohibited by the Civil Rights Act of 1964 on the basis of:

    a.   Sex, race, color, religion, and national origin.

    b.   Age, sex, race, color, or religion.

    c.   Age, physical handicap, race, color, and religion.

    d.   Age, physical handicap, race, color, and national origin.

6._____   A policy of the EEOC is:

    a.   To restrict enforcement of employment discrimination laws to relatively small companies to minimize disruptions.

    b.   To regulate comparable worth statutes enacted by the states.

    c.   Never to resort to legal remedies to achieve the goals of the EEOC.

    d.   To have businesses achieve employment mixes more closely reflecting the local minority and female labor pool.

7._____   Which federal statute does not apply to discrimination in employment?

    a.   The Americans with Disabilities Act.

    b.   Occupational Safety and Health Act of 1970.

    c.   Pregnancy Discrimination Act.

    d.   Title VII of the Civil Rights Act of 1964.

8._____   Government contractors in employment may discriminate on the basis of:

    a.   race.

    b.   religion.

    c.   ability.

    d.   sex.

9.____   Affirmative action programs to promote employment of members of minority groups may:

    a.   Impose hiring and promotion quotas with regard to members of an under represented class.

    b.   Require that older employees be fired to hire younger affirmative action employees.

    c.   Not discriminate on the basis of race or sex.

    d.   Not create training programs for minority employees to help them in the workplace.

10.____   Practices subject to Title VII of the Civil Rights Act of 1964 include:

    a.   Compensation and fringe benefits but not retirement plans.

    b.   Job taking, classifications, and assignments but not union discrimination.

    c.   Any term, condition, or privilege of employment.

    d.   Hiring and discharge of employees but not promotions.

MATCHING

a.   <u>McDonnell-Douglas Corp. v. Green</u>

b.   <u>Price Waterhouse v. Hopkins</u>

c.   Executive Order 11246

d.   Hostile work environment

e.   Americans with Disabilities Act

f.   <u>Espinoza v. Farah Manufacturing</u>

g.   <u>U.S. v. Paradise</u>

h.   ADA Enforcement Guidance

i.   School Board of Nassau County, Florida v. Arline

j.   Johnson v. Minnesota Historical Society

k.   Johnson v. Transportation Agency, Santa Clara County, California

1.   Older Workers Benefit Protection Act

m.   Disparate impact

n.   Griggs v. Duke Power Company

o.   Reasonable accommodations

p.   Bona fide occupational qualification

q.   Civil Rights Act of 1991

r.   McDonald v. Santa Fe Trail Transportation Company

s.   United States v. Seeger

t.   Harris v. Forklift Systems, Inc.

1._____   This is a form of sexual harassment involving deliberate, repeated and unwelcome sexual advances.

2._____   Describes the situation in which an employer does not actively engage in discrimination against an individual or a group of individuals on the basis of race, color, religion, sex, or national origin, but the effect of being neutral on such basis is to cause a disproportionally adverse impact.

3._____   This law permitted an employer to observe a bona fide employee benefit plan for incentives for early retirement.

4._____   States that discrimination is permitted in instances in which sex, religion, or national origin (but not race) is reasonably necessary to the normal operation of that particular business.

5._____   This case held that employers who engage in sex stereotyping may be liable for discrimination.

6._____   This act amended Title VII to equalize the damage awards in most discrimination suits.

7._____   This requires government contractors to adopt affirmative action.

8._____   This act expands the rights of disabled persons to employment opportunities and public access.

9._____   This case held that the term "national origin" in Title VII refers to the country where a person is born or the country from which his or her ancestors came.

10._____   This case held that a District Court impose a goal of 25% black employees at all ranks.

11._____   This case held that if the risk of infecting children with tuberculosis is slight, the infected person should be reinstated, otherwise she must be considered for another assignment.

12._____   This case held that age might have been an impermissible factor under the ADEA.

13._____   This lists prohibited disability-related questions.

14._____   This case upheld the legality of an affirmative action plan, noting that such a moderate, flexible, case-by-case approach is consistent with Title VII, for it allows an employer to voluntarily eliminate the vestiges of discrimination.

15._____   This case held that conduct that a reasonable person would find hostile or abusive is illegal.

16._____   This case broadly defined the term "religion" used in Title VII to require only a sincere and meaningful belief, occupying in the life of its possessor a place parallel to that filled by the God of those religions generally recognized.

17._____   This case held that Title VII protected whites against racial discrimination when a black employee, who along with a white employee misappropriated their employer's property, was only reprimanded while the white was discharged.

18._____   This is the standard which employers must meet in modifying the workplace for qualified disabled employees.

19._____   This case set out the four-part test that a plaintiff must meet to prove a prima facie case of discrimination.

20._____   This case held that neutral employment criteria will be judged by their impact, not by the good or bad faith involved in their implementation.

CASE PROBLEMS

1.   The airplane manufacturer laid off a group of workers, in a business slow down, including Mr. Brown, an African American. While he was out of work, he joined a civil rights protest outside of the plant gates, participating in a demonstration that prevented trucks from entering and leaving company property. When business picked up and the plant called back its former workers, it did not call back Mr. Brown. He filed a complaint with the EEOC for racial discrimination. What is his best argument, and what is the best defense for the employer?

_____

_____

_____

2.   Women who worked as secretaries in the Alabama prison system applied to become jail guards because the guards position was paid more money than the clerical positions. They were denied because they could not meet the height and weight requirements for the guards position. What is their best argument to put on a prima facie case of sex discrimination? What is the state's best defense?

_____

_____

_____

3.   Brian Weber, a white, was employed by Kaiser Aluminum. Kaiser and the union that represented its employees agreed that half of the new participants in a training program would be black until the proportion of black workers was increased in certain job categories. Weber was denied entry to the program in favor of black applicants who were less qualified than he and had less seniority. Weber sued, claiming that he was a victim of racial discrimination under Title VII. What is the best defense for Kaiser and the union?

_____

_____

_____

4.   Mrs. Newsome worked as a secretary for C-W Manufacturing Company at its No. 3 plant, where Mr. Evans had also once worked. Several years earlier, he had been transferred and demoted from that plant for his aggressive and abrasive conduct toward female employees. However, the plant management believed that he had been rehabilitated, and brought him back to No. 3. While there, he asked Mrs. Newsome for a date. She refused and tried to avoid him. He began to sit on the corner of her desk, telling off-color jokes, and spreading his legs open in front of her. She complained to her boss, who told her not to worry. The behavior continued, she became more stressed, and complained again. She was told to be quiet or quit. On that she filed a complaint with the EEOC. What is her best argument? What is the manager's best defense?

_____

_____

_____

5.   Ellen is a supervisor of nurses at Park View Hospital, and has been there for most of her career. She has received many merit pay increases over the last twenty years, and is now one of the more highly paid members of the hospital nursing staff. The hospital management is in a budget crunch and needs to cut costs. One of its options is to terminate highly paid positions. When Ellen's position is considered, what issues should management include in its strategic planning?

_____

_____

_____

APPLICATION QUESTIONS

Bundy v. Jackson

United States Court of Appeals, D. C. Circuit
641 F.2d 934 (1981)

Facts and Background. Sandra Bundy was a Vocational Rehabilitation Specialist with the District of Columbia Department of Corrections (the agency). She achieved her GS-9 level one year after she filed her formal complaint of sexual harassment with the agency. Beginning in 1972 she received and rejected sexual advancements from Delbert Jackson, a fellow employee and currently the agency's Director. In 1974, the sexual intimidation Bundy suffered began to intertwine directly with her employment, when she received constant propositions from two of her supervisors. The District court refused to grant her any relief, while finding that "the making of improper sexual advances to female employees [was] standard operating procedure, a fact of life, a normal condition of employment." The court found that her supervisors did not take the "game" of sexually propositioning female employees "seriously" and concluded that sexual harassment does not in itself represent discrimination "with" respect to . . . terms, conditions, or privileges of employment" within the meaning of Title VI. Bundy appealed.

Judge J. Skelly Wright delivered the opinion of the court.

***

In Barnes v. Castle . . . we held that an employer who abolished a female employee's job to retaliate against the employee's resistance to his sexual advances violated Title VII of the Civil Right Act of 1964. The appellant in this case . . . asks us to extend Barnes by holding that an employer violates Title VII merely by subjecting female employees to sexual harassment, even if the employee's resistance does not cause the employer to deprive her of any tangible job benefits.

***

[O]ur task of statutory construction in <u>Barnes</u> was to determine whether the disparate treatment Barnes suffered was "based on... sex." We heard arguments that whatever harm Barnes suffered was not sex discrimination, since Barnes' supervisor terminated her job because she refused sexual advances, and not because she was a woman. We rejected those arguments as disingenuous in the extreme. The supervisor in that case made demands of Barnes that he would not have made of male employees. "But for her womanhood . . . [Barnes'] participation in sexual activity would never have been solicited. To say, then, that she was victimized in her employment simply because she declined the invitation is to ignore the asserted fact that she was invited only because she was a woman subordinate to the inviter in the hierarchy of agency personnel. . . .

We thus made it clear in <u>Barnes</u> that sex discrimination within the meaning of Title VII is not limited to disparate treatment founded solely or categorically on gender. Rather, discrimination is <u>sex</u> discrimination whenever sex is for no legitimate reason a substantial factor in the discrimination.

We thus have no difficulty inferring that Bundy suffered discrimination on the basis of sex...[We have no difficulty ascribing the harassment--the "standard operating procedure"--to Bundy's employer, the agency. Although Delbert Jackson himself appears not to have used his position as Director to harass Bundy, an employer is liable for discriminatory acts committed by supervisory personnel, and there is obviously no dispute that the men who harassed Bundy were her supervisors. Delbert Jackson and other officials in the agency who had some control over employment and promotion decisions had full notice of harassment and did virtually nothing to stop or even investigate the practice. We thus readily conclude that Bundy's employer discriminated against her on the basis of sex. What remains is the novel question whether the sexual harassment of the sort Bundy suffered amounted by itself to sex discrimination with respect to the <u>"terms, conditions, or privileges of employment."</u> Though no court has as yet so held, we believe that an affirmative answer follows ineluctably from numerous cases finding Title VII violations whether an employer created or condoned a substantially discriminatory work <u>environment</u>, regardless of whether the complaining employee lost any tangible job benefits as a result of the discrimination.

Bundy's claim on this score is essentially that "conditions of employment" include the psychological and emotional work environment--that the sexually stereotyped insults and demeaning propositions to which she was indisputably subjected and which caused her anxiety and debilitation, illegally poisoned that environment.

***

[Poisoning the atmosphere of employment . . . violates Title VII. [S]exual harassment... injects the most demeaning sexual stereotypes into the general work environment and always represents an intentional assault on an individual's innermost privacy.

***

Indeed, so long as women remain inferiors in the employment hierarchy, they may have little recourse against harassment beyond the legal recourse Bundy seeks in this case.

***

Bundy proved that she was the victim of a practice of sexual harassment and a discriminatory work environment permitted by her employer. Her rights under Title VII were therefore violated.

***

The "Guidelines [on Sexual Harassment in the Workplace" issued by the Equal Employment Opportunity Commission] . . . affirm that an employer is responsible for discriminatory acts of its agents and supervisory employees with respect to sexual harassment just as with other forms of discrimination, regardless of whether the employer authorized or knew or even should have known of the acts, and also remains responsible for sexual harassment committed by nonsupervisory employees if the employer authorized, knew of, or should have known of the harassment. The general goal of these Guidelines is _preventive_.

***

Applying these Guidelines to the present case, we believe that the director of the agency should be ordered to raise affirmatively the subject of sexual harassment with all employees and inform all employees that sexual harassment violates Title VII of the Civil Rights Act of 1964, [and] the Guidelines of the EEOC. The director should also establish and publicize a scheme whereby harassed employees may complain to the director immediately and confidentially. The director should promptly take all necessary steps to investigate and correct any harassment, including warnings and appropriate discipline directed at the offending party, and should generally develop other means of preventing harassment within the agency.

Perhaps the most important part of the preventive remedy will be a prompt and effective procedure for hearing, adjudicating, and remedying complaints of   sexual harassment within the agency....Finally, the agency must inform any employee denied relief within the agency of his or her right to file a civil action in the district court.

CASE QUESTIONS

1.   Does Title VII apply to federal employees?

_____

_____

_____

2.   How did the court define sex discrimination?

_____

_____

_____

3.   Did the court find that the employer was liable for the sexual discrimination of Bundy's supervisors?

_____

_____

_____

4.   Could employer liability for one employee's sexual harassment of another employee be considered based on the doctrine of respondent superior?

_____

_____

_____

5.   Did the court conclude that there was sexual harassment even though there was no loss
      of tangible job benefits?

      _____

      _____

      _____

CH. 17 - Environmental Law

OVERVIEW AND CHAPTER OUTLINE

This chapter begins with a discussion of common law rules that regulate environmental quality, and the application of nuisance and trespass law. It examines the major federal laws enacted to protect the environment, including the EPA, the Clean Air Act, Clean Water Act, Resource Conservation and Recovery Act, the Superfund, and the Endangered Species Act. It concludes with a section on global environmental issues and international cooperative efforts.

I.   **POLLUTION AND THE COMMON LAW**

    A.   Nuisance Law and Pollution

    B.   Trespass and Pollution

    C.   Negligence, Strict Liability and Pollution

    D.   Water Rights and Pollution

II. **FEDERAL ENVIRONMENTAL PROTECTION**

III. **CLEAN AIR ACT**

    A.   National Ambient Air Quality Standards

    B.   State Implementation Plans

    C.   The Permit System

        1.   Clean Air Areas

        2.   Dirty Air Areas

        3.   The Bubble Concept

    D.   Mobile Sources of Pollution

        1.   International Perspectives: Auto Emission Controls in Europe

    E.   Toxic Pollutants

    F.   Acid Rain

    G.   Enforcement

        1.   Carrot-and-stick Approach

IV.   CLEAN WATER ACT

    A.   Point Source Pollution

        1.   Industrial Permits

            a.   Control Technology

    B.   Enforcement

    C.   Nonpoint Source Pollution

    D.   Wetlands

        1.   Permit System

        2.   Wetlands Takings

V.   LAND POLLUTION

    A.   Toxic Substances Control Act

    B.   Pesticides

    C.   Resource Conservation and Recovery Act

KEY WORDS AND PHRASES

Public nuisance
Private nuisance
Trespass
Negligence
Strict liability for abnormally
    dangerous activities
Riparian water law
The Silent Spring
Clean Air Act of 1970
National Ambient Air Quality
    Standards (NAAQS)
State Implementation Plan (SIP)
Attainment areas
Prevention of Significant
    Deterioration (PSD) areas
Maximum allowable increase
Best Available Control
    Technology (BACT)
Nonattainment areas
Emissions offset policy
Lowest Achievable Emissions
    Rate Technology (LAER)
Net air quality improvement
Bubble concept
Minimum emissions rates (MERS)
Bleifrei
Acid rain
Citizen suits
Permit
Navigable waters
Point source
Publicly owned treatment
    works (POTWs)

National Pollutant Discharge
    Elimination System (NPDES)
Best conventional technology (BCT)
Best available technology (BAT)
New source performance
    standards (NSPS)
Discharge monitoring reports (DMRs)
Nonpoint sources
Wetlands
Toxic Substances Control
    Act (TOSCA)
Biotechnology
Federal Insecticide, Fungicide,
    and Rodenticide Act (FIFRA)
Resource Conservation and
    Recovery Act (RCRA)
Hazardous waste
Manifest system
Manifest
National Priority List
Comprehensive Environmental
    Response, Compensation and
    Liability Act (CERCLA)
The Superfund
Superfund Amendments and
    Reauthorization Act (SARA)
Strictly and jointly and severally liable
Endangered Species Act (ESA)
Endangered species
Montreal Protocol
Pollution Prevention Act of 1990

FILL-INS

1._____   This act sharply increased federal authority to control air pollution.

2._____   Is responsible for the regulation of pollutants generated by industry that are transmitted to the external environment.

3._____   This requires managers to complete and record a detailed form that sets out the nature of the hazardous waste and identifies its origin, routing, and final destination.

4._____   An EPA strategy which treats all facilities within one industrial complex as a single emission source.

5._____   This book focused public attention on the dangerous use of pesticides during the 1960's.

6._____   A substantial and unreasonable interference with the use and enjoyment of the land of another.

7._____   These require plants in Dirty Air areas to use the lowest achievable emissions rate technology.

8._____   In finding liability under this common law theory, courts generally emphasize the risks created by the toxic pollutant and the location of the business relative to population centers.

9._____   It requires industrial polluters to list the amount and type of their discharges, subject to a permit application process.

10._____   It presents a public welfare concern when toxic substances seep into the groundwater from runoffs and leaks in underground tanks.

11._____   Every unauthorized and direct breach of the boundaries of another's land.

12._____   An international treaty in which richer nations agree to pay poorer nations not to pollute, in order to reduce total CFC emissions into the ozone.

13._____   A solid waste which because of its quantity, concentration, or physical, chemical, or infectious nature may cause or pose a substantial present or potential hazard to human health or environment.

14._____   New plants in Clean Air areas must use the best available control technology to control and reduce air pollution, under these standards.

15._____   An unreasonable interference with a right held in common by the general public.

16._____   The release of CFCs into this layer has caused a decrease in the upper atmosphere which may cause massive increases in skin cancer.

17._____   These plans are concerned with air pollution problems caused by tailpipe emissions and hazardous air pollutants.

18._____   It is funded through a surtax on those businesses with an annual income in excess of $2 million in the petroleum and chemical feedstocks industries.

19._____   This air pollutant, sulfuric and nitric acid, comes from burning coal and oil to produce electricity.

20._____   Unlike the Clean Air Act, this Act does not impose separate pollution control requirements on newly constructed plants, but requires all industries to have a permit for effluents.

MULTIPLE CHOICE QUESTIONS

Select the best answer to each of the following questions.

1.____   Which of the following Acts is <u>not</u> directly concerned with water quality?

   a.   The Clean Water Act.

   b.   Resource Conservation And Recovery Act.

   c.   River and Harbor Act.

   d.   Safe Drinking Waters Act.

2.____   Which of the following are <u>not</u> factors in the willingness of Congress to subject environmental pollution to federal regulation?

   a.   Rachel Carson's book, <u>Silent Spring.</u>

   b.   The snail darter case in the Tennessee Valley Authority.

   c.   The court's decision in <u>Boomer v. Atlantic Cement</u>.

   d.   All of the above.

   e.   None of the above.

3.____   To bring an action to have a polluter declared a public nuisance which of the following is <u>not</u> necessary?

   a.   Plaintiff must prove that there has been an unreasonable interference with a right held in common by the general public.

   b.   Plaintiff must prove that the pollution affects many people.

   c.   Plaintiff must prove that the polluter acted intentionally.

   d.   Plaintiff may be part of a class, and the suit may be brought in the community's name by the city attorney.

4._____ In bringing a common law trespass action, plaintiff must prove all of the following except that:

a. There was an unauthorized breach of the boundaries of plaintiff's land.

b. There was a tangible invasion of plaintiff's land.

c. That the invasion was direct.

d. No efforts were being made by the defendant to stop the trespass.

5._____ Early federal efforts at regulating environmental protection failed because:

a. The states were doing such a good job that Congress felt they should remain in control of protecting the environment.

b. Congress felt that there was no problem.

c. Private litigation was a satisfactory means of protecting the environment.

d. Federal laws over relied on the abilities of state and local governments to regulate environmental quality.

6._____ Which is not one of the four basic types of environmental pollution which the Environmental Protection Agency is required to control?

a. Water pollution.

b. Land pollution.

c. Worker exposure to toxins in the workplace.

d. Air pollution.

7._____   Which of the following is <u>not</u> true about the Global Response to environmental pollution?

    a.   The less developed nations want all pollution to cease, no matter what the cost.

    b.   The less developed nations want the industrialized nations to pay them for their rights to pollute.

    c.   The Montreal Protocol is a treaty freezing CFC levels.

    d.   The cost of environmental clean up in East Germany is expected to be over $100 billion.

8._____   Which of the following is true about the <u>Georgia v. Tennessee Copper Co.</u> case?

    a.   It held that polluters provided so many jobs and other benefits to a region that the only penalty for trespass or nuisance should be damages, not an injunction.

    b.   It proclaimed that gas pollution moving across state lines was subject to an injunction.

    c.   It proclaimed that pollution was no longer a state concern but rather was now a federal matter.

    d.   It has affected virtually every major project, both public and private, since its enactment.

9._____   Which of the following has generally <u>not</u> been one of the options open to a court when a common law nuisance action is brought?

    a.   The polluter could be ordered to pay damages to the injured plaintiff.

    b.   The polluter could be permitted to continue polluting.

    c.   The polluter could be ordered to engage in research to develop a better technology to ultimately reduce or eliminate the pollution.

    d.   The polluter could be sent to prison.

10.____   All of the following factors inherent in the judicial system made private litigation an ineffective means of protecting the environment, except:

   a.   The judicial system lacks the ability to monitor pollution and its control.

   b.   Courts are very pro-business and often refused to permit plaintiffs to file actions against large polluters.

   c.   Judges generally lack the scientific, technical, and economic expertise required to impose the appropriate level of pollution control in nuisance actions.

   d.   Only where pollution impacts a party with a significant economic interest to protect will a common law case even develop.

   e.   All of the above are factors.

MATCHING

Match the following terms or phrases to the descriptions below.

a.   Pollution Prevention Act of 1990

b.   Clean Air Act of 1970, as amended

c.   Bradley v. American Smelting and Refining Co.

d.   Comprehensive Environmental Response, Compensation, and Liability Act

e.   Chevron v. NRDC

f.   Wetlands

g.   Prevention of Significant Deterioration areas

h.   Mobile source emission standards

i.   Nonattainment areas

j.   Toxic Substances Control Act

k.   National Pollution Discharge Elimination System

l.   <u>Quivira Mining Co. v. EPA</u>

m.   <u>Branch v. Western Petroleum</u>

n.   <u>Babbitt v. Sweet Home</u>

o.   Endangered Species Act

p.   <u>Arkansas v. Oklahoma</u>

q.   Joint and several liability

r.   National Ambient Air Quality Standards

s.   State Implementation Plan

t.   Clean Water Act

1._____   Areas that have not achieved national air quality standards.

2._____   The stated purpose of the Act is to "restore and maintain" the quality of the nation's water resources.

3._____   Federal Act that attempted to strengthen the federal role in air pollution by specifying an orderly procedure for the adoption and achievement of ambient air quality standards by the states.

4._____   This case held that the EPA can force a state to accept lower water quality standards than it chooses.

5._____   This case considered whether toxic air pollutants could give rise to actions in both trespass and nuisance.

6._____   The name the Clean Water Act gives to the permit system covering the technology requirements and the effluent limitations imposed on individual plants.

7._____   A federal law recognizing the need to preserve endangered species and to manage on an ecosystem scale.

8._____   This law encourages businesses and government agencies to consider and plan for all aspects of pollution reduction through every phase of their operations.

9._____   This case upheld the Bubble Concept as a proper "statutory source" for measuring and regulating air pollution.

10._____   This case held that an industrial polluter who discharges liquid chemical wastes upon the ground is strictly liable for any injuries resulting from the contamination of the ground water.

11._____   Under this theory each of the parties could be liable for the entire costs notwithstanding the fact that she/he may have contributed only a fraction of the total hazardous waste to the site.

12._____   They were intended to define the specific control efforts necessary within the state to achieve the national air quality standards.

13._____   Determined on the basis of public health and welfare effects, these specified standards to be uniformly applied across the nation.

14._____   These environmentally important areas include swamps and bogs.

15._____   These areas include national parks, wilderness acres, national monuments, and other areas where the air quality is better than the level specified by national standards.

16._____   They were suspended when it was found that the technology available to meet the hydrocarbon monoxide standards would significantly increase emissions of sulfuric acid.

17._____   Provides a regulatory mechanism to protect the public against dangerous chemical materials contained in consumer and industrial products.

18._____   Superfund.

19._____   The court ruled that logging must cease on government lands until the loggers offered a plan to avoid harm to the northern spotted owl and red-cockaded woodpecker.

20._____   The court held that even though a waterway may not be navigable itself, if pollutants discharged into it can affect interstate commerce, the waterway will fall under the Clean Water Act.

CASE PROBLEMS

1.   Atlantic Richfield was assessed penalties that included paying the cost of cleaning up oil discharges from an accidental oil spill. Atlantic argues that imposing the penalties constituted a criminal action and argue that if they are not given a jury trial, they will be denied due process. Should they be given a jury trial?

_____

_____

_____

2.   Union Electric Co. was unable to comply with emission levels set by the State of Missouri that were more stringent than federal regulations. Union Electric sued the EPA, challenging the approval of standards that were economically or technologically infeasible. Can the EPA consider economic or technological infeasibility in evaluating an emission standard?

_____

_____

_____

3.   Atlantic Cement had invested more than $45 million in a cement manufacturing plant that employed over 300 people. A group of nearby landowners sought an injunction to stop the operation of the plant and sought damages for their injuries caused by dirt, smoke, and vibration from Atlantic's operations. Should the court close down the plant?

_____

_____

_____

4. American Can Co. sued the State of Oregon alleging that an Oregon statute violated equal protection as an unwarranted interference with interstate commerce. The statute prohibited the use of nonreturnable containers for beer and carbonated beverages and prohibited the sale of metal beverage containers that used detachable pull-top opening devices as being an environmental pollutant. Should the statute be declared unconstitutional?

    _____

    _____

    _____

5. Under authority of the Toxic Substances Control Act, the EPA issued regulations requiring Dow Chemical, among other companies, to submit to the EPA lists of studies initiated by the company on ten chemicals suspected of being hazardous. Dow challenged the requirement claiming that it would be a disincentive to companies to conduct research. Should the EPA regulation be overturned?

    _____

    _____

    _____

APPLICATION QUESTIONS

DO YOU AGREE OR DISAGREE WITH THE FOLLOWING STATEMENTS? JOT DOWN YOUR REASONS.

1. Under the Clean Air Act, one polluter can buy a right to pollute from another industry which is already operating in nonattainment areas.

    Agree _____   Disagree _____

    Reasons:

2.   If a plant wishes to locate in a clean air (PSD) area, it must use the LAER standard.

Agree _____   Disagree _____

Reasons:

3.   The bubble concept applies to all of the buildings and facilities in any geographic area, so that emissions offsets may be traded among all the firms operating there.

Agree _____   Disagree _____

Reasons:

4.   The Clean Water Act is directed to point sources of pollution from industry, but has largely left unregulated the water pollution caused by liquid waste discharge from cities.

Agree _____   Disagree _____

Reasons:

5.   If Alpha Manufacturer produces a chemical which is used in Printers' Ink
      Company's product, and which creates a liquid waste hazardous to the public, the
      chemical must be documented and tracked with complete records from the time of
      production to ultimate disposal. This is required under RCRA's manifest system.

      Agree _____   Disagree _____

      Reasons:

6.   The Endangered Species Act is not a part of the Environmental Protection policy in
      the U.S., and as such, has little effect on business and economic development.

      Agree _____   Disagree _____

      Reasons:

CH. 18 - Consumer Protection

OVERVIEW AND CHAPTER OUTLINE

This chapter summarizes and discusses several consumer protection laws enacted by the federal government and the federal agencies designated to implement and enforce those laws. These include the areas of food and drug safety, deceptive advertising and marketing practices, and consumer credit protection.

I.   **THE FDA: FOOD AND DRUG REGULATION**

    A.   Food Safety

        1.   FDA Powers Expanded in the 1930s

        2.   Food Additives: The Delaney Clause

    B.   Nutrition Labeling

        1.   Nutrients by Serving Size

        2.   Standards for Health Claims

    C.   Drug Safety

        1.   Designation of Prescription Drugs

KEY WORDS AND PHRASES

Food and Drug Administration (FDA)
The Jungle
Food, Drug and Cosmetic Act of 1938
Delaney Clause
Nutrition Labeling and Education
   Act of 1990
Prescription Drugs
Kefauver Amendment of 1962
Proven effectiveness
Learned intermediary doctrine
Unfair and deceptive
Consent decree
Deceptive
Deception policy statement
Unfair
Advertising substantiation program
Lanham Act
Trade regulation rules
Federal Register
R-value Rule
Mail Order Rule
Used Car Rule
Magnuson-Moss Warranty Act
Written warranties

Full warranty
Limited warranty
Consumer Credit Protection
   Act (CCPA)
Truth-in-Lending Act (TILA)
Disclosure
Annual percentage rate
Regulation Z
Consumer Leasing Act
Fair Credit Billing Act (FCBA)
Fair Credit Reporting Act (FCRA)
Credit bureaus
Consumer credit reports
Equal Credit Opportunity
   Act (ECOA)
Credit discrimination
Prohibited bases
Regulation B
Written notification
Debt collection agency
Fair Debt Collection Practices Act
Electronic fund transfer services
Electronic Fund Transfer Act
Regulation E

FILL-INS

1._____   A new act intended to prevent food product labels from being misleading and to help consumers make informed purchases.

2._____   Summarizes a three-part test to give the FTC staff guidance on its investigation of deceptive products.

3._____   Can be used to shield a drug manufacturer from injuries caused when a doctor ignores instructions and changed recommended dosage.

4._____   Requires advertisers and advertising agencies to have a reasonable basis before they disseminate claims.

5._____   Requires that every proposed drug must be FDA approved, not only with respect to safety but with respect to its effectiveness for that purpose.

6._____   Under this rule, a company offering to sell merchandise by mail must have a reasonable basis for expecting to ship the merchandise within the time stated in the solicitation.

7._____   Rules designed to set boundaries on certain acts and practices that the FTC believes to be subject to deception.

8._____   Defines food additives and gives the FDA the authority to license the use and to set the safe use-level of additives.

9._____   Agreements signed by both the parties charged in a complaint and by a majority of the commissioners of the FTC.

10._____   Requires that warranties be reasonably clear, simple, and useful.

11._____   This Act prohibits the marketing of any drug until the FDA approves the application submitted by the manufacturer.

12._____   This regulation provides specific rules explaining what constitutes unlawful discrimination under the ECOA.

13._____   The requirement that standardized terms in consumer leasing provisions be given to consumers.

14._____ Requires credit bureaus to adopt practices for meeting businesses' needs for consumer information in a manner fair and equitable to the consumer.

15._____ Requires that specific standardized loan terms be given to consumers before they become committed to a credit transaction.

16._____ Provides the basic framework establishing the rights, liabilities, and responsibilities of participants in electronic fund transfer systems.

17._____ It is essentially an umbrella act for the federal regulation of consumer credit markets.

18._____ It provides standard disclosure terms to help consumer shop around for leases.

19._____ This book caused public controversy with its graphic criticism of food safety control.

20._____ This Act regulated the conduct of independent debt collectors but does not apply to creditors attempting to collect their own debts.

21._____ This Act establishes procedures to dispute billing errors and to report lost or stolen credit cards.

MULTIPLE CHOICE QUESTIONS

Select the best answer to each of the following.

1._____ The Federal Trade Commission would most likely file a suit against a business firm:

a. Which attempts to increase its sales by cutting its prices on certain goods.

b. Engaged in false or deceptive advertising.

c. Which refused to buy from certain companies.

d. Which failed to meet safety standards in the production of its products.

2._____   Which of the following does the Federal Trade Commission not have the power to do:

    a.   Prosecute criminal actions.

    b.   Issue a consent order or a cease and desist order.

    c.   Make rules in the area of advertising.

    d.   Investigate misleading advertising and deceptive practices.

3._____   The FTC sometimes files suit after a seller has made false or deceptive advertising claims. Which of the following is correct concerning advertising regulation?

    a.   The seller must have a reasonable basis for its advertising.

    b.   The number of people deceived does not necessarily determine if ad deception existed.

    c.   The FTC can order corrective advertising.

    d.   The FTC investigates activities suspected to be unfair.

    e.   All of the above.

4._____   What items does the Federal Trade Commission not look to in determining whether advertisers have a reasonable basis for advertising claims?

    a.   Consequences of a false claim.

    b.   Benefits of a truthful claim.

    c.   Amount of substantiation experts in the field believe is reasonable.

    d.   The advertising medium chosen by the seller.

5._____   Which is true of the Delaney Clause?

    a.   Every proposed drug must be FDA approved.

    b.   Drugs must be approved not only respect to safety but with respect to its effectiveness for the purpose sold.

    c.   FDA must approve human clinical testing of drugs.

    d.   Defines food additives and gives the FDA authority to license the use and set the safe use level of additives.

6._____   Which of the following was not enacted as a part of or as an amendment to the Consumer Credit Protection Act?

    a.   Truth-in Lending Act.

    b.   Fair Credit Reporting.

    c.   Uniform Consumer Credit Code.

    d.   Equal Credit Opportunity Act

7._____   Which of the following is not prohibited by the Equal Credit Opportunity Act?

    a.   Denial of credit based on lack of assets.

    b.   Discrimination based on receipt of public benefits such as welfare.

    c.   Denial of credit based on the sex of the applicant.

    d.   Denial of credit based on the marital status of the applicant.

8._____   The purpose of the Truth-in-Lending Act is to:

    a.   Limit the interest rate that can be charged on consumer credit transactions.

    b.   Provide procedures for consumers to settle billing problems.

    c.   Assure a meaningful disclosure of credit terms to encourage competition in the financing of consumer credit.

    d.   Limit the amount a debtor can be made to pay monthly per creditor.

9._____   Which of the following is not a provision of the Fair Credit Billing Act?

    a.   Credit cards may not be distributed to persons who have not applied for them.

    b.   A credit card holder cannot be liable for more than $50 if the card is stolen or lost.

    c.   A credit card issuer must place a notice on the consumer contract that any holder is subject to the consumer's defenses against the seller.

    d.   Consumers must notify the creditor within 60 days of the first billing of the disputed charge.

10._____   Under the Fair Debt Collection Practices Act, which is the correct provision?

    a.   Debt collectors may petition the court to garnish wages of the debtors.

    b.   Creditors may sell the debt to a collection agency.

    c.   Debt collection agencies may not discuss the debt with the debtor's employer.

    d.   All of the above.

MATCHING

Match the following terms or phrases to the descriptions below.

a.   The Lanham Act

b.   Insulation R-Value Rule

c.   Gammon v. GC Services

d.   Orkin Exterminating Company

e.   United States v. Park

f.   Food Additives Amendment of 1958

g.   Tobin v. Astra Pharmaceutical Products

h.   Magnuson-Moss Federal Warranty Act

i.   Used Car Rule

j.   Nutrition Labeling and Education Act of 1990

k.   Fair Debt Collection Practices Act

l.   Truth-in-Lending Act

m.   Fair Credit Billing Act

n.   Equal Credit Opportunity Act

o.   Automated teller machines

p.   Consumer Credit Protection Act

q.   Consumer Leasing Act

r.   Fair Credit Reporting Act

s.   Regulation Z

t.   Regulation B

1._____   Held that executives of companies covered by the Food, Drug, and Cosmetic Act could be held responsible for compliance with the Act.

2._____   This court used the "unsophisticated consumer" standard to find possible false claims by a debt collector.

3._____   A court ruled that this company had unfairly raised the annual renewal fees for its contracts, violating an agreement with its customers.

4._____   Is the FTC's Trade Regulation Rule Concerning the Labeling and Advertising of Home Insulation.

5._____   Known as the "Delaney Clause".

6._____   This Act requires companies to label foods so that nutrition is shown by serving size, and to correct a lack of nutrition education that may be partly responsible for poor diets.

7._____   The court refused to allow FDA drug approval to preempt state product liability claims on design defect.

8._____   Is the federal government's effort to provide meaningful warranties.

9._____   This Act permits private civil actions for false or misleading advertising.

10._____   Required dealers to disclose warranty terms and known defects on a sticker pasted in the window of each car offered for sale.

11._____   Known as twenty-four-hour tellers, they enable consumers to perform a variety of banking transactions.

12._____   Prohibits discrimination against applicants for credit on the basis of race, sex, color, religion, national origin, and marital status.

13._____   Written by the Federal Reserve Board to implement the Truth-in-Lending Act and specifies items that are part of the finance charge.

14._____   With its passage, Congress became actively involved in regulating the direct relationship between the consumer and the creditor.

15._____   The object of this statute is to encourage consumers to shop around for the most favorable credit terms.

16.____   Established standardized terms to be disclosed in consumer leases of personal property.

17.____   Established procedures for customers when credit cards are lost or stolen or when monthly credit card statements contain billing errors or disputed charges.

18.____   Protects consumers against harassment and other unfair or deceptive practices and requires the debt collector to send certain information within five days of the initial contact with the debtor.

19.____   Requires credit bureaus to adopt practices for consumer information in a manner fair and equitable to the consumer.

20.____   Regulation that provides specific rules for determining what constitutes unlawful credit discrimination.

CASE PROBLEMS

1.   Palmetto Foods, a manufacturer of baby foods, was inspected by the FDA and given written notice that rats were found throughout its facilities. A year later, the FDA came again and found that conditions had not improved. Can anyone be criminally prosecuted for these failings?

_____

_____

_____

2.   Green received a new credit card that she solicited from King Department Store. A burglar broke into her apartment and stole the credit card. She notified King of the theft two days later. Using the credit card, the burglar made a $500 purchase the day before she notified King and a $499 purchase the day after she notified King. Discuss her liability for these charges.

_____

_____

_____

3.   Palmer wants to insulate his roof, but doesn't know how to tell the difference between kinds of insulation. He wonders if there is any consumer protection rule to help him, and if there is, what it is. Can you help him?

_____

_____

_____

4.   Mary Smith purchased a car from Don Chapman Motor Sales, paying some money down and signing a contract to pay the remainder of the price in 36 monthly installments. The credit agreement failed to state the APR. Now that Mary has been laid off due to a plant closing she can no longer pay her bills as they come due. What are her options, if any?

_____

_____

_____

5.   Virginia wants to package her "cheese straws," a snack food for consumer sales. What must the label show?

_____

_____

_____

APPLICATION QUESTIONS

DO YOU AGREE OR DISAGREE WITH FOLLOWING QUESTIONS? JOT DOWN YOUR REASONS.

1.   Corporate managers of food companies are sheltered from criminal liability if they do not personally know about adulteration of foodstuffs within their businesses.

Agree _____   Disagree _____

Reasons:

2.   If Mother Millie is required to have little Millicent vaccinated against measles before entering school, and even if the drug should cause a severe adverse reaction, there is no legal recourse when the FDA has approved the drug for use.

Agree _____   Disagree _____

Reasons:

3.   The FDA requires too much testing before drugs are allowed to be marketed, increasing the cost and delaying availability of the product. Congress should require the FDA to leave drug safety to the market place and the doctrine of strict liability.

Agree _____   Disagree _____

Reasons:

4.   It was proposed that FTC findings be based on a three part test: the presence or omission of information likely to mislead a reasonable consumer to the detriment of the consumer. The reasonableness of the consumer would be determined by age, health, or other demographic characteristic, so that some business activities could be held to higher standards of care than others. This is discriminatory behavior which the courts have not allowed.

Agree _____   Disagree _____

Reasons:

5.   A well known TV personality was paid to use Skinny Minnie's Diet Plan, and advertise her weight loss success on her nationally watched program. Lumpy Linda saw the actress lose weight, and believed that she could lose weight also. What she did not see was that the actress followed a strict regimen of exercise each day. This is deception that is actionable under the FTC.

Agree _____   Disagree _____

Reasons:

CH. 19 - Antitrust Law

OVERVIEW AND CHAPTER OUTLINE

This chapter discusses the development and application of antitrust laws intended to regulate horizontal and vertical business arrangements. The chapter presents a discussion of antitrust common law, the antitrust statutes, the interpretation of the statutes by the courts, and the enforcement policies of the administrative agencies. It includes vertical restraints of trade among buying and selling firms in the business chain.

I.   **ANTITRUST COMMON LAW**

II. **THE ANTITRUST STATUTES**

    A.   The Sherman Act

    B.   The Clayton Act

    C.   The Federal Trade Commission Act

III. **EXEMPTIONS FROM AND ENFORCEMENT OF THE ANTITRUST LAWS**

    A.   Exemptions

    B.   Enforcement

        1.   Sherman Act

        2.   Clayton Act

2.   Volume Discounts Legal?

B.   Defenses

XVI. **SUMMARY**

XVII. **ISSUE: HOW STABLE ARE JAPAN'S CARTELS?**

KEY WORDS AND PHRASES

Restrain competition
Injure competitors
Restraints of trade
Sherman Antitrust Act
Antitrust
Clayton Act
Federal Trade Commission Act
Unfair methods of competition
State action doctrine
Criminal felonies
Injunction
Treble damages
Per se rule
Horizontal restraint of trade
Japanese cargo system
Merger
Horizontal merger
Merger guidelines
Market power
Market share
Product market
Geographic market

Relevant market
Potential competitors
Failing firm defense
Power-buyer defense
Per se illegal
Rule of reason
Horizontal price fixing
Territorial allocations
Vertical restraints of trade
Resale price maintenance (RPM)
Territorial restrictions
Customer restrictions
Tying arrangement
Tie-in sale
Vertical Restraint Guidelines (1985)
Boycott
Robinson-Patman Act
Price discrimination
Predatory pricing
Cost justification
Meeting competition

FILL-INS

1. _____ This approach is used to determine whether a business practice will automatically be held to be illegal under the antitrust laws by the courts.

2. _____ Is the term used to describe a business where tasks making up the production process are performed in-house or by contract.

3. _____ Congress passed this Act to supplement the Sherman Act after Supreme Court decisions had limited its application.

4. _____ Were issued by the Department of Justice and the Federal Trade Commission to reduce the uncertainty associated with the enforcement of the antitrust laws by increasing the predictability of when mergers are likely to be challenged and the factors that will be considered.

5. _____ If they are harmed by a violation of the Sherman Act, they can sue for treble damages. If they win, they get three times their actual money damages, plus court costs and attorneys' fees.

6. _____ The Clayton Act refers to this in the phrase "any section of the country." Its determination is fundamental in determining the legality of a merger.

7. _____ Shares jurisdiction, with the Justice Department in Clayton Act matters, and can issue cease and desist orders, investigate suspect business dealings, hold hearings, and issue an administrative order requesting a discontinuance or modification of certain business acts.

8. _____ In order to determine this when deciding the legality of a merger, the court must take into account the appropriate product and geographic markets.

9. _____ Was enacted by Congress in 1914 to prohibit specific business practices that substantially lessened competition or tend to create a monopoly.

10. _____ Merger between businesses that are on the same level of the market and generally in the same market.

11. _____ This approach to determine whether a business practice is illegal means that the Courts will look at the facts surrounding the agreement, arrangement, or other restraint before deciding whether it helps or hurts competition.

12. _____   An Act of Congress that specifically exempts insurance companies from antitrust law.

13. _____   Is the name given to a collection of firms that come together by contract or other form of agreement in an attempt to restrain trade by restricting output and raising prices.

14. _____   Is a defense to a merger that was created by the courts and not provided by statute and can be used by firms that are not likely to survive without the merger.

15. _____   Was passed by Congress in 1890 as a unified federal response to anticompetitive practices.

16. _____   This term is used to define a group of businesses operating at the same level, which come together through contract, merger or conspiracy.

17. _____   The Japanese practice of prior consultation among bidders on public works jobs.

18. _____   This act provides that unfair methods of competition in or affecting commerce, and unfair or deceptive acts or practices in commerce are illegal.

19. _____   Generally involves an agreement between a manufacturer, its wholesalers, distributors of other suppliers, and the retailers that is intended to control the price at which the product is sold to consumers.

20. _____   Supreme Court decision forbidding resale price maintenance agreements under antitrust laws.

21. _____   Supreme Court decision that a vertical restraint is not illegal per se.

22. _____   Like the fair trade laws, it was enacted to protect high-cost distributors from price-cutting competition and price discrimination.

23. _____   A form of price discrimination based on the size of the purchase.

24. _____   The Court has had little to say about them, giving little reason to suspect that the standard for approval of such mergers would be significantly different from the standard for horizontal mergers.

25. _____   This occurs when a manufacturer sells the same product to different buyers at different prices.

26. _____   Under one explanation for the existence of resale price maintenance agreements, where this is present, retailers impose a resale price maintenance arrangement on the manufacturer. The manufacturer then serves to monitor cheating.

27. _____   Antitrust violation that occurs when a group conspires to force compliance with a price fixing scheme.

28. _____   A firm operating in two markets and charging different prices could be in violation of antitrust law unless it can establish this defense.

29. _____   The ability of a company to affect market prices of the products of its own and of other companies.

30. _____   Business practices designed to exclude competitors indirectly from the market, making it more difficult for competitors to challenge the market power of the aggressive firm.

31. _____   An agreement by a party to sell one product but only on the condition that the buyer also purchases a different product, or at least that he will not purchase that product from any other supplier.

32. _____   A firm operating in two markets could be in violation of antitrust law if it dropped its price in response to a competitor who cut their price first if it weren't for this defense.

33. _____   Restricts a business to delivery in a designated area, with any delivery outside the territory permitting the manufacturer to revoke the franchise agreement.

MULTIPLE CHOICE QUESTIONS

Select the best answer to each of the following questions.

1. _____   Which of the following is an **incorrect** statement concerning actions for violating antitrust laws?

      a.   Both the Department of Justice and private parties may initiate civil proceedings.

      b.   The FTC may issue cease and desist orders.

      c.   Serious violations can result in company assets being impounded by The Federal Trade Commission for sale to compensate injured consumers.

      d.   The FTC may issue immunity to antitrust prosecution to firms who ban together for export trade.

2. _____   Which of the following is likely to stop a merger?

      a.   The merger would allow the firm to increase its market share sufficiently to be able to affect the price of the product.

      b.   The merger would reduce that amount of business information collected and disseminated by the industry trade association, thereby decreasing competition.

      c.   Although the two merging firms make entirely different products, competition is reduced because they are potential competitors.

      d.   All of the above are correct.

      e.   Only a and c are correct.

3. _____   What pricing agreements among competitors are legal?

    a.   An agreement that is aimed at lowering prices.

    b.   None because competitors are forbidden to enter into agreements that determine the price of the product they sell.

    c.   An agreement that is aimed at ending cutthroat competition by stabilizing prices.

    d.   An agreement that seeks to fix prices fairly and reasonably for the benefit of consumers.

4. _____   With regard to federal antitrust laws:

    a.   They are dynamic, changing as society changes.

    b.   They are enforced only in geographic markets.

    c.   They reached the antitrust activity of the OPEC cartel.

    d.   They forbid only mergers.

5. _____   The Standard Oil of New Jersey decision:

    a.   Held that all contracts in restraint of trade were per se illegal.

    b.   Found that Standard Oil had violated the Clayton Act.

    c.   Defined the relevant market.

    d.   Established the rule of reason.

6. _____   The U.S. Justice Department's merger guidelines are:

   a.   Strongly influenced by the size of the market share of the parties to the proposed merger.

   b.   Based exclusively upon the decisions of the United States Supreme Court.

   c.   Binding on all parties affected by them.

   d.   Not of great importance. They are too indefinite and uncertain.

7. _____   The ABC Company has been charged with an "attempt to monopolize" the small appliance industry. ABC will be able to defeat this charge if it can prove that:

   a.   It does not have monopoly power.

   b.   Its activities do not constitute an unreasonable restraint of trade.

   c.   Its percentage share of the relevant market was less than 50%.

   d.   It did not intend to monopolize the industry.

8. _____   Which of the following is not specifically prohibited by the Clayton Act:

   a.   Price discrimination where such might tend substantially to lessen competition.

   b.   Mergers which might tend substantially to lessen competition.

   c.   Monopolizing, attempt to monopolize, or conspiracy to monopolize.

   d.   Being a director of two or more major, competing corporations where elimination of competition would be a violation of antitrust laws.

9. _____   The Sherman Act is <u>not</u> directed at trade restraints involving:

    a.   Contracts and combinations.

    b.   Attempts to monopolize.

    c.   Monopolization.

    d.   Price discrimination.

10. _____   Several firms competing in Kansas reached an agreement to divide up the market on a county-by-county basis. Each firm agreed not to sell to customers outside their territory. In addition, the firms agreed to fix their prices. The courts will likely:

    a.   According to the Court's decision in <u>Sealy</u>, find the agreement per se illegal.

    b.   According to the Court's decision in <u>Sealy</u>, apply the rule of reason to determine the effect of the agreement on competition.

    c.   According to the Court's decision in <u>Brown Shoe</u>, find that the agreement is illegal because it constitutes a contractual horizontal merger.

    d.   According to the Court's decision in <u>Brown Shoe</u>, find the agreement legal because it does not violate the Clayton Act.

11. _____   Mark Corp. has been charged with a violation of the Robinson-Patman Act. To establish a violation, it is necessary to show that:

    a.   Mark made sales of goods of a like grade and quality to two or more customers at different prices.

    b.   A monopoly resulted.

    c.   Mark profited from the alleged violation.

    d.   An actual lessening of competition occurred.

12. _____   Which of the following in a correct statement concerning tying arrangement under the Clayton Act?

    a.   Test of whether a tying arrangement is illegal is essentially the same as for vertical price fixing.

    b.   Test of whether a tying arrangement is illegal is essentially the same as under the Sherman Act.

    c.   It is not illegal under Clayton Act because it is not covered by the Clayton Act.

    d.   It is not illegal if the tied goods are not sold in the United States.

13. _____   Johnson Corp. has obtained a patent on a revolutionary coin operated washing machine. It is far superior to existing machines currently in use. Which actions do not constitute a violation of federal antitrust law?

    a.   Maintaining resale price for machines it sells to distributors.

    b.   Obtaining a near total monopolization of the market as a result of the patent.

    c.   Requiring purchases of the machines to buy all there washing supplies from Johnson.

    d.   Joining in a boycott with other appliance manufacturers to eliminate a troublesome discount distributor.

14. _____   Smith Corp. entered into a contract to supply all the requirements of 1,000 dealers in the South. The dealers agreed not to sell products competitive with those of Smith. These dealers constituted 20% of the total number of dealers in the area. Smith may:

    a.   Be enjoined from enforcing the contracts if they might substantially lessen competition.

    b.   Be enjoined only to the extent that its own outlets operated by its agents are involved.

    c.   Not be enjoined because less than 50% of dealers in the South are involved.

    d.   Be enjoined for violating the Robinson-Patman Act.

15. _____   In Albrecht v. Herald Co., the Supreme Court held:

    a.   Minimum retail prices may not be fixed by a wholesaler or producer.

    b.   Maximum retail prices may not be fixed by a wholesaler or producer.

    c.   Minimum, but not maximum, retail prices may be fixed by a wholesaler or producer.

    d.   Retail trade associations may fix either minimum or maximum prices.

16. _____   In FTC v. SCTLA, the Court held:

    a.   There was no violation of the Sherman Act.

    b.   There was no boycott to fix prices.

    c.   The per se rule applies only to concerted actions on nonprice restrictions.

    d.   SCTLA was liable for the conspiracy to set prices through a boycott under both the Sherman and Clayton Acts.

17. _____   Dixon Corp. manufactures a patented, high quality product. It discovers that discount stores are using it as a loss leader. Dixon has commenced a rigorous enforcement of its suggested minimum retail price. Dixon is:

   a.   In violation of the Robinson-Patman Act.

   b.   Engaging in illegal price fixing under the Clayton Act.

   c.   Not in any violation of antitrust law.

   d.   Not in violation of antitrust law since Dixon was seeking to protect a patented product.

18. _____   Twice Co. produces high quality clocks that are sold in competition with clocks of other manufacturers. It sells only to dealers who agree to Twice's pricing policies. Several other manufacturers have similar marketing arrangements. This arrangement is:

   a.   Legal, Twice is merely meeting the competition as in <u>Albrecht</u>.

   b.   Legal as a permissible resale price maintenance agreement.

   c.   Illegal under <u>Dr. Miles</u>.

   d.   Legal, since Twice is merely trying to keep, his company profitable.

19. _____   With regard to federal antitrust laws, vertical mergers are:

   a.   Exempt if they do not tend to monopolize or lessen competition.

   b.   Exempt according to the Vertical Merger Guidelines.

   c.   Covered to a lesser extent than all horizontal mergers.

   d.   Covered to the extent determined only by the FTC.

20. _____   Territorial restrictions:

        a.   Are an example of horizontal territorial restraint

        b.   Are common among car manufacturers.

        c.   Involve a contractual relationship between the manufacturer and the retailer under which the retailer agrees not to sell rival manufacturer's products within the retailer's product market.

        d.   Are commonly used by soft drink companies.

        e.   Answers b and d are correct.

MATCHING *(Horizontal Arrangements)*

Match the following terms or phrase to the description below.

a.   International Shoe v. FTC

b.   U.S. v. Philadelphia National Bank

c.   U.S. v. General Dynamics Corp.

d.   U.S. v. Baker Hughes

e.   Standard Oil Company of New Jersey v. U.S.

f.   Broadcast Music. Inc. v. CBS

g.   NCAA v. Board of Regents of University of Oklahoma

h.   Brunswick Corp. v. Pueblo Bowl-O-Mat

i.   U.S. v. Sealey Inc.

j.   U.S. v. United States Gypsum Co.

k.   FTC v. Indiana Federation of Dentists

l.   Copperweld v. Independence Tube

m.   <u>U.S. v. El Paso Natural Gas Co.</u>

n.   A per se rule

o.   A rule of reason

p.   Export Trading Company Act

q.   <u>FTC v. Proctor & Gamble Co.</u>

r.   <u>Northern Pacific Railroad Co. v. United States</u>

s.   <u>U.S. v. Trenton Potteries</u>

t.   <u>Arizona v. Maricopa County Medical Society</u>

1. _____   Forced a divestiture where two strong companies sought to merge, finding that
                it was relevant to consider potential competitors and not just sellers currently
                in the same market.

2. _____   A rule of law that operates automatically, without the necessity of further
                proof.

3. _____   The case in which the Supreme Court enunciated the failing firm defense.

4. _____   This case allowed a merger where powerful buyers had sufficient bargaining
                power to ensure that the merged firm could not charge monopoly prices.

5. _____   Forced the dissolution of a trust composed of many firms so that the firms
                would compete as individual entities.

6. _____   One of the classic antitrust cases condemning direct price fixing as an
                unreasonable <u>per se</u> restraint of trade under the Sherman Act.

7. _____   This case held that the geographic market is generally limited to areas where
                consumers can reasonably be expected to make purchases.

8. _____   Held that a merger of a large household products maker and the leading
                manufacturer of liquid bleach could not occur because the household products
                maker was a potential manufacturer of bleach.

9. _____   An act granting a limited exemption from antitrust prosecution to firms which work together to export their products.

10. _____   A rule of law requiring the court to look at the facts surrounding an action.

11. _____   The case that appeared to mark a turning point in standards the Supreme Court set for striking down mergers, requiring the government to demonstrate more economic damage to competition than it had been required to in the past.

12. _____   Applied a "rule of reason" to a case involving price fixing, finding that a blanket license issued by the parties did not constitute per se illegal price fixing.

13. _____   The court held that where territorial limitations are part of "an aggregation of trade restraints," they violate Section 1 of the Sherman Act.

14. _____   This case held that, while the rule of reason might be applied, information sharing was generally an indefensible practice.

15. _____   This case held that one company with its subsidiaries was incapable of conspiring to violate the antitrust laws.

16. _____   Held that certain actions are per se illegal where, because of their pernicious effect on competition and lack of any redeeming virtue, are conclusively presumed to be unreasonable.

17. _____   Held that a maximum fee arrangement established by foundations formed by two medical societies were price- fixing agreements and were per se illegal.

18. _____   Held that under a "rule of reason" analysis, an association could not fix prices colleges would receive for television appearances made by their football teams.

19. _____   This case held that firms whose profits fall because a new competitor enters the market cannot sue for damages because increased competition is favored, not frowned upon, by antitrust law.

20. _____   Held that the FTC was justified in attacking the policy of a dentists' organization requiring members to withhold x-rays from dental insurance companies.

MATCHING *(Vertical Arrangements)*

Match the following terms or phrase to the description below.

a.   Boycott

b.   Predatory pricing

c.   <u>Continental T.V. v. GTE Sylvania</u>

d.   Resale price maintenance

e.   Consumer restrictions

f.   <u>Eastern States Retail Lumber Dealers Assn. v. U.S.</u>

g.   <u>Business Electronics Corp. v. Sharp Electronics Corp.</u>

h.   <u>Eastman Kodak Co. v. Image Technical Services, Inc.</u>

i.   Vertical Restraint Guidelines of 1985

j.   <u>FTC v. Superior Court Trial Lawyers Association</u>

k.   <u>Albrecht v. Herald Company</u>

l.   <u>White Motor Company v. United States</u>

m.   <u>United States Steel Corporation v. Fortner Enterprises</u>

n.   <u>Jefferson Parish Hospital District No. 2 v. Hyde</u>

o.   <u>Texaco v. Hasbrouck</u>

p.   Robinson-Patman Act

q.   Tied product market

r.   <u>Dr. Miles Medical Company v. John D. Park & Sons Company</u>

s.   <u>Northern Pacific Railway Company v. United States</u>

t.   Price differentials

1. _____   This occurs when a group conspires to prevent the carrying on of business or to harm a business, often used in a price fixing scheme.

2. _____   Held that a contract between a hospital and a professional medical corporation requiring all anesthesiological services for the hospital's patients to be performed by that firm did not violate the Sherman Act.

3. _____   Held that because a company did not have appreciable economic power in the market for credit, under a rule of reason analysis a tie-in arrangement did not exploit monopoly power.

4. _____   This is an agreement between a manufacturer, supplier, and retailers of a product under which the retailers agree to sell the product at not less than a minimum price.

5. _____   Held that restricting truck dealers to selling only in a specified area around their dealerships was not a per se violation of antitrust laws and adopted a rule of reason.

6. _____   This case adopted the per se rule and found that a manufacturer of medicines violated antitrust law by setting minimum prices.

7. _____   This case defined an agreement by a party to sell one product but only on condition that the buyer also purchases a different product, or at least agrees that he will not purchase that product from any other supplier.

8. _____   The market for a product which must be purchased or sold with a second product.

9. _____   These may be imposed on suppliers by manufacturers when the manufacturer elects to sell directly to a certain customer category.

10. _____   Vertical pricing arrangements that create artificially low prices which may benefit consumers but have adverse effects on competition.

11. _____   These differences in prices of the same product to different buyers are not necessarily illegal.

12. _____   The Supreme Court held that it is illegal price discrimination to sell the same good at different prices to different customers, unless there are legally permissible cost differentials.

13. _____   Case holding that manufacturers have wide latitude in selecting dealers who will agree to follow the marketing strategies of the parent company.

14. _____   A Supreme Court decision allowing an issue of the illegality of a tie-in arrangement involving parts and service to go to a jury.

15. _____   The Justice Department's three tests for imposition of a _per_ _se_ rule of antitrust illegality.

16. _____   Held that in addition to the _Dr. Miles_ prohibitions against fixing minimum retail prices, a manufacturer or supplier may not fix maximum retail price.

17. _____   An act which includes an anti-chain store section for the purpose of protecting single-store competitors.

18. _____   Upheld territorial restrictions imposed by the manufacturer, holding that territorial restraints may be considered under a rule of reason analysis, considering interbrand competition more important than intrabrand competition.

19. _____   Struck down a boycott designed to punish lumber wholesalers who sold directly to the public.

20. _____   Held that the boycott by a professional lawyers group doing public criminal defense work was illegal _per_ _se_.

CASE PROBLEMS

1.   Assume that an American company operating in France is accused of conspiring to monopolize some aspect of the American market. This activity, however, does not violate French antitrust law. May the U.S. Department of Justice prosecute this claim?

_____

_____

_____

2.   Assume the following market shares are held by brewery manufacturers: Low Beer, 25%; High Beer, 20%; Near Beer, 15%; Sweet Beer, 10%; Sour Beer, 10%; Swell Beer, 10%; Smear Beer, 5%; and Dear Beer, 5%. Is the Department of Justice likely to challenge a merger of Dear Beer and Smear Beer?

_____

_____

_____

3.   A group of small hardware stores want to create one company to act as a buying agent so that members could buy products in bulk and receive larger discounts. Should they form themselves into one company, or may they proceed through an agreement among themselves as separate firms?

_____

_____

_____

4.   Marsh Machinery builds bulldozers. Prior to 1981, it sold on credit a substantial amount of equipment to Hale Contractors. Hale went into bankruptcy in 1981. In order to protect its investment, Marsh took over Hale's business. Johnson Contractors now complains that the acquisition harms its business, on the ground that its business would have improved had Marsh not entered the market as a competitor. Can Johnson recover damages from Marsh?

_____

_____

_____

5.   During the 1980's, many different companies merged, creating vertically integrated firms. Why was this not stopped in court under the antitrust laws?

_____

_____

_____

6.   When "Hungry Herman's" charged $.89 a gallon for gas to its customers in City A, and $.94 a gallon to its customers in City B, it was charged with price discrimination. Does "HH" have any defenses?

_____

_____

_____

APPLICATION QUESTIONS

DO YOU AGREE OR DISAGREE WITH THE FOLLOWING STATEMENTS?   JOT DOWN YOUR REASONS.

1.   Arnie, Butch, and Chan entered into an agreement with Donnie to conduct their separate businesses as though there were no agreement, while at the same time charging all their customers the same prices. Donnie ultimately refused to go along with the others and started selling his grain below the agreed upon price. The court will enforce the agreement for the benefit of Arnie, Butch and Chan, under the common law of contracts.

      Agree _____   Disagree _____

      Reasons:

2.   If Paul's Paint Shop requires its customers to buy Bristle Brushes in order to purchase Paul's paints, this is a tying contract which may violate the Sherman Act.

      Agree _____   Disagree _____

      Reasons:

3.   In #1 above, if Arnie, Butch, Chan, and Donnie conducted their uniform pricing agreement under the terms of the Sherman Act, the courts would probably not find it a per se violation unless it were unreasonable.

Agree _____   Disagree _____

Reasons:

4.   If Sun Racer, a new U. S. Auto manufacturer, decides to purchase its batteries from one supplier according to a contract, it has decided to integrate its business with a potentially opportunistic firm.

Agree _____   Disagree _____

Reasons:

5.   At the beginning of the summer travel season, the U.S. airline companies entered into a price war for domestic flights, with each seeking to set its price slightly below that of its competitors, with a blatant attempt to increase market share and drive competitors out of the market. This is a per se price fixing violation.

Agree _____   Disagree _____

Reasons:

6.   If the tire manufacturer, the tire distributor, and the tire retailer agree to sell prices to the consumer at a certain minimum price, they have engaged in a vertical price fixing arrangement.

        Agree _____   Disagree _____

        Reasons:

7.   Manufacturers can force a resale price maintenance agreement on retailers, but retailers cannot force a RPM on manufacturers.

        Agree _____   Disagree _____

        Reasons:

8.   Ben and Jerry's Ice Cream Company has agreed to grant two franchises for retail sales in the county around State University. Both dealers know what the usual price per serving is, but one cuts its prices to increase its sales. If the other retailer is harmed economically by this price cut, it can demand that Ben and Jerry's terminate the rival's franchise.

        Agree _____   Disagree _____

        Reasons:

9.   When Lane's Shoe Co. offers its customers at the annual shoe sale a chance to "buy three and get one free," it is clearly tying the shoes in violation of the Sherman Act.

Agree ____   Disagree ____

Reasons:

10.   If the National Chemical Workers Union goes on strike against We Mean to Clean, Inc., it can urge that other unions, customers and suppliers join it in a boycott against We Mean and its horizontal competitors, until unsafe working conditions are rectified. Such a boycott of the other firms can be a per se violation of the Clayton Act.

Agree ____   Disagree ____

Reasons:

CH. 20 - Securities Regulation

OVERVIEW AND CHAPTER OUTLINE

This chapter develops the concept of a security and discusses the past and present regulation of securities and securities markets. The chapter explains the major aspects of the 1933 and 1934 securities laws, the cornerstone of regulation of new investment opportunities. The disclosure requirements of the 1934 securities law to prevent fraud are also covered. The chapter concludes with a discussion of investment companies, investment advisors, and stock market regulation.

I. **CORPORATE FINANCE AND EARLY REGULATION**

    A. Securities and Corporate Finance

        1. Debt

        2. Equity

    B. Origins of Securities Regulation

        1. Beginnings of Federal Regulation

        2. The Securities and Exchange Commission

II. **DEFINING A SECURITY**

    A. Supreme Court's <u>Howey</u> Test

        1. Defining the Four Elements

KEY WORDS AND PHRASES

Security
Debt
Equity ownership
Debt financing
Equity financing
Blue sky laws
Securities and Exchange
    Commission (SEC)
Howey Test
Investment of money
Common enterprise
Undivided interest
Expectation that profits will
    be generated by the efforts
    of persons other than the investor
Disclose
Material information
Registration statement
Prospectus
Red herring
Merits
Stop order
Shelf registration
Underwriter
Exemption from registration
Initial sale
Private placement
Accredited investors
Over-the-counter (OTC)
Publicly held company
Private company
10-K annual report

Quarterly 10-K reports
8-K reports
Proxy
Tender offer
Securities fraud
Misleading statements
Material omissions
Material misinformation
Safe harbor
Insider trading
Fiduciary duty
Insider Trading Sanctions
    Act of 1984
Insider Trading and Securities
    Fraud Enforcement Act of 1988
Investment Company Act (ICA) of 1940
Investment company
Open-end company
Mutual fund
Load
No-load
Registration and Disclosure
Conflicts of interest
Investment advisors
Investment Advisors Act (IAA)
Brokers
Dealers
Securities professionals
Churning
Adequate information
Specialist firms

FILL-INS

1._____   Immunity from suit for corporate forecasts.

2._____   Holds that for something to be a security there must be an investment of money; a common enterprise; and the expectation that profits will be generated by the efforts of persons other than the investor.

3._____   Name attached to state securities laws.

4._____   Condenses the longer registration statements that are provided to the SEC.

5._____   Those presumed sophisticated enough to evaluate investment opportunities without the benefit of an SEC approved prospectus.

6._____   An extensive audited document that must be filed annually and is similar in content to the information provided when registering securities under the 1933 Act.

7._____   Enacted to reduce the uncertainty of what will qualify as a private placement.

8._____   Adopted by the SEC to enforce the Securities Acts, this rule provides for liability for using any manipulative or deceptive device in the purchase or sale of securities.

9._____   Permits a company to propose a new security offering that meets all registration requirements, without having to sell all of the securities at one time.

10._____   The investment banker who markets a new security.

11._____   Mutual fund, offered directly to the public through the mail with no sales commission.

12._____   An entity engaged primarily in the business of investing or trading in securities.

13._____   Firms that generally do not deal directly with the public, handling transactions for brokers.

14._____   Those with access to nonpublic information.

15._____   Establish and enforce rules of conduct for their members, including how securities are listed and obligations of issuers of securities.

16._____   Was passed by Congress to give the SEC a clear statutory basis for prosecuting insider trading.

17._____   The dispute resolution procedure used to settle claims against brokers and dealers.

18._____   This market is composed of securities dealers, and the stocks traded on this market are from firms that have a relatively small number of shares of stock or are themselves relatively small.

19._____   An offer made to stock owners in a target company of stock in the acquiring company or cash in exchange for their stock.

20._____   Was created by the 1934 Act establishing an association responsible for preventing fraud among OTC brokers and dealers.

MULTIPLE CHOICE QUESTIONS

Select the best answer to each of the following questions.

1._____   Which of the following is subject to the registration requirements of the Securities Act of 1933?

    a.   Public sale of bonds by a municipality.

    b.   Public sale by a corporation of its negotiable 10 year notes.

    c.   Public sale of stock issued by a common carrier regulated by the Interstate Commerce Commission.

    d.   Stock issued by a charitable foundation.

2._____   A primary purpose of the Securities Act of 1933 is to:

    a.   Make certain that investors receive fair value when they buy stock.

    b.   Advise investors so they can make informed investment decisions.

    c.   Detect and prevent fraud in the sale of securities.

    d.   Prevent the offering of securities thought to be unsound.

3._____   Which of the following is correct regarding qualification for the private placement exemption from registration under the 1933 Act?

    a.   The instrumentalities of interstate commerce must not be used.

    b.   Securities must be offered to not more than 35 persons.

    c.   The minimum amount of securities purchased by each offeree must not be less than $1,000,000.

    d.   Investors must have access to or be furnished with the kind of information that would be available in a registration statement.

4._____   All of the following are elements of a security except:

    a.   An investment of money.

    b.   A common enterprise.

    c.   The expectation that profits will be generated by the efforts of persons other than the investor.

    d.   The expectation that profits will be generated primarily by the efforts of the investor.

    e.   All of the above are elements.

5._____   Securities available under a private placement made pursuant to Regulation D of the Securities Act of 1933:

a.   Must be sold to accredited institutional investors only.

b.   Must be sold to less than 25 unaccredited investors.

c.   Are subject to restrictions on their resale.

d.   Cannot be subject to payment of commissions.

e.   Are exempt from the Disclosure restrictions in Rule 10 b (5).

6._____   Proxy solicitation:

a.   Is basically unregulated.

b.   Is regulated by the Securities Act of 1933.

c.   Is controlled by the Securities and Exchange Commission.

d.   Is prohibited.

7._____   Stock markets:

a.   may regulate and police their own members.

b.   may decide who may handle certain transactions and who may not.

c.   may determine how prices are set and reported.

d.   all of the above.

e.   a and b only.

8._____   An investment company:

      a.   Is essentially not regulated by the federal government and only subject to state blue-sky laws.

      b.   Was regulated as a result of Congress ordering the FTC to study investment companies.

      c.   Refers to any corporation that takes more than 25% of its assets in a corporation listed on the New York Stock Exchange (NYSE).

      d.   Is an entity engaged in the business of trading in securities and is regulated by the SEC pursuant to the Investment Company Act of 1940.

9._____   Investment newsletters and their publishers:

      a.   Are controlled and regulated by the 1934 Securities Exchange Act.

      b.   Constitute the sale of an investment, making its author subject to Rule 10b-5 if there is a knowing violation of the 1933 Securities Act.

      c.   Are investment advisers under the IAA.

      d.   Are not investment advisers regulated by the IAA.

10._____   The Insider Trading Sanctions Act:

      a.   Was passed by Congress to give the SEC a clear statutory basis for prosecuting insider trading.

      b.   Codified the Chiarella decision.

      c.   Does not permit the imposition of treble damages.

      d.   Has not been used by the SEC which considered it too weak to tackle the problem of major deals by insiders affecting the securities markets.

MATCHING

Match the following terms or phrases to the descriptions below.

a.   Shelf registration

b.   Debt financing

c.   Equity financing

d.   1934 Securities Act

e.   Share of stock

f.   1933 Securities Act

g.   Private placement exemption

h.   Prospectus

i.   <u>Reves v. Ernst & Young</u>

j.   Load funds

k.   <u>Dirks v. SEC</u>

l.   <u>CTS Corp. v. Dynamics Corp. of America</u>

m.   <u>Basic Inc. v. Levinson</u>

n.   Churning

o.   Security

p.   <u>Chiarella v. United States</u>

q.   Investment Advisers Act

r.   <u>Lowe v. SEC</u>

s.   Brokers

t.   Securities Litigation Reform Act of 1995

1._____   A claim on the future profits of a company.

2._____   Involves selling bonds or borrowing money by contract.

3._____   Allows corporations to "dribble" stock into the market in an attempt to manage the price received for the shares.

4._____   First act of Congress to adopt regulations concerning the sale of securities.

5._____   A corporation raises funds through the sale of its stock.

6._____   Federal law which regulates securities after issuance.

7._____   Written instrument evidencing either debt or ownership.

8._____   Held that a promissory note could be a security if it met the Howey test.

9._____   The offering document that must be provided to every buyer of securities according to the 1933 Act.

10._____   The kind of mutual fund sold to the public through a securities dealer which has a sales commission of some percent of the price.

11._____   Held that publishers of investment newsletters are not investment advisers under the IAA.

12._____   A person engaged in the business of effecting transactions in securities for the account of others.

13._____   This law limits the liability of accountants and underwriters to the proportion of securities fraud for which they are found responsible.

14._____   Held that a broker-dealer who discovered fraud in a company and revealed this information to his clients was not guilty of insider trading.

15._____   Held that the Williams Act did not preempt a state takeover statute and that the state statute did not violate the Commerce Clause.

16._____   A corporation that is exempt from registration under the SEC with fewer than thirty-five investors and whose stock is not publicly traded.

17._____   Is complementary to the ICA and defines investment adviser.

18._____   A case holding that a misrepresentation is material if it would have been significant to a reasonable investor.

19._____   Held that a printer at a company that printed financial documents who read some confidential information and traded on it was not a corporate insider and could not be charged with securities fraud.

20._____   This occurs when a broker sells an excessive amount of stock primarily to make money from the commissions earned in other transactions.

CASE PROBLEMS

1.   Borak was a shareholder of a corporation who sued when it merged with another corporation on the grounds of breach of fiduciary duty, because of misrepresentations contained in management's proxies. Borak also sued to invalidate the merger. On what grounds may Borak state his cause of action?

_____

_____

_____

2.   Manor Drug sued Blue Chip Stamp under Section 10(b) and Rule 10b-5 of the 1934 Act for damages based on allegedly pessimistic statements in a prospectus sent to Manor Drug. Relying on these statements, Manor Drug did not purchase Blue Chip stock. Can a nonpurchaser of stock sue for damages in a private suit, or is 10b-5's coverage limited only to actual buyers or sellers of securities?

_____

_____

_____

3.   Anderson was the president of Jones Development Corp., a company engaged in the exploration of oil and gas deposits. He gave a press conference, after his stock began to rise on the basis of rumors of the finding of a rich oil deposit. He denied that there had been a stock find. When the ore discovery was subsequently revealed, he was sued for violation of the securities laws. Will he be found liable?

_____

_____

_____

4.   John and Martha Retirees were persuaded by Slick Billy Broker to invest $20,000 in stock of Company A, not knowing that Billy had just purchased shares in that company which he needed to unload on the buyers for a nice profit. They ultimately lost their investment and want to sue Billy. Do they have any remedies?

_____

_____

_____

5.   South Dakota adopted a statute requiring any entity owning a substantial percent of the stock in a corporation incorporated and doing business in that state to comply with the state statute regulating hostile takeovers. Johnson, the president of Blase Corporation, felt that the South Dakota statute was too restrictive and sued claiming that the state had been preempted by the Williams Act from prohibiting such an action, making the South Dakota statute unconstitutional. How would a court rule? Why?

_____

_____

_____

APPLICATION QUESTIONS

DO YOU AGREE OR DISAGREE WITH THE FOLLOWING STATEMENTS? JOT DOWN YOUR REASONS.

1.   Michael Milkem tried to find investors for his new Junkque, Enterprises, and told prospective purchasers of securities that he had conditional sales contracts already in his hands that would more than cover the value of their investments. In fact, this was not the case, and the investors lost their money. This is an example of a material misstatement under the 1934 Act.

Agree ____   Disagree ____

Reasons:

2.   Michael Milkem tried again with another group of investors, but this time he was smarter. He told them nothing about the anticipated success of the proposed venture, but secretly encouraged rumors that he was on to a "sure thing," and was going to make a great deal of money. If the investors were foolish enough to believe rumors, they deserved to lose their money, and the 1934 Act will not protect them.

Agree ____   Disagree ____

Reasons:

3.   Ivan's Investment Firm dropped a hint that a remarkable new biotechnical process was about to be marketed that would revolutionize the clean up of oil spills. This made the price of his company's stock soar, so that when he was ready to sell it, he made a fortune. Immediately thereafter, another firm came out with the patent for the process, and the price of his stock dropped dramatically. Many investors who had recently purchased the shares lost a great deal of their equity position. This will not cause Ivan to be liable for misstatement because the investors could have checked out his story more closely.

Agree _____   Disagree _____

Reasons:

4.   Ginny wants a secure and flexible way to invest in the stock market, so she chooses a mutual fund with a load provision. This means that she must agree to buy a specified amount of stocks before the company will take her on as a client.

Agree _____   Disagree _____

Reasons:

5.   Investors really like the binding arbitration provisions that they sign when establishing accounts with investment firms, because it means that they do not have to go before juries, should their investments fail through the mismanagement or fraud of their brokers.

Agree _____   Disagree _____

Reasons:

CH. 21 - The International Legal Environment of Business

OVERVIEW AND CHAPTER OUTLINE

This chapter provides an overview of the international legal environment of business, beginning with the nature of it and the ways the U.S. government works to restrict imports and stimulate exports. Next, it considers various forms available to a business involved in an international commercial venture. It reviews the constraints imposed by the Foreign Corrupt Practices Act. It continues with a discussion about international contracting and insurance, and concludes with dispute resolution procedures.

I. **THE NATURE OF INTERNATIONAL BUSINESS**

    A. The International Business Environment

    B. Risks in International Business Transactions

II. **INTERNATIONAL LAW**

    A. History of International Law

    B. Sources of International Law

    C. International Trade Agreements

        1. North American Free Trade Agreement

        2. World Trade Organization

III.   **U.S. IMPORT RESTRICTIONS AND PROMOTIONS**

    A.   Taxes on Imports

        1.   Tariff Classes

        2.   Harmonized Tariff Schedules

        3.   Bans on Certain Products

    B.   Import Price Controls

        1.   Antidumping Orders

        2.   Countervailing Duties

            a.   Certain Subsidies Allowed

        3.   Foreign Trade Zones and Duty-Free Ports

    C.   Export Regulation and Promotion

        1.   Juris*prudence*? A Bargain -- Only $29.35 for a Razor Blade!

        2.   Federal Government Efforts

        3.   State Government Efforts

        4.   Export Restrictions

            a.   Licensing Agreements

            b.   Application to Reexported U.S. Goods

            c.   Penalty Provisions

        4.   International Perspectives: Controlling International Pirates

IV.   **BUSINESS ORGANIZATIONS IN FOREIGN MARKETS**

    A.   Exporting Manufactured Products

    B.   Foreign Manufacturing

        1.   Wholly Owned Subsidiary

        2.   Joint Venture

        3.   Licensing Agreement

KEY WORDS AND PHRASES

International business
International business environment
Financial, political, and
   regulatory risks
Lex mercatoria
North American Free
   Trade Agreement (NAFTA)
General Agreement on
   Tariffs and Trade (GATT)
World Trade Organization (WTO)
Tariff
Special tariffs
Ad valorem tariffs
Tariff schedules
Entireties
Harmonized Tariff Schedule
International Trade Administration (ITA)
International Trade Commission (ITC)
Dumping

Antidumping Duty Act
Countervailing duty laws
Foreign trade zones
Duty-free ports
Trade deficit
Export Trading Company Act
Export Administration Act
Licensing agreements
Validated license
Qualified general license
General license
Commodity Control List
Application to reexported goods
Export
Indirect exporting
Direct exporting
Wholly owned subsidiary
Joint venture
Licensing agreement (contract)

Franchising	Forum selection clause
Foreign Corrupt Practices Act (FCPA)	Choice-of-law clause
International contract	Nationalization
Meishi	Expropriation
Letter of credit	Confiscation
Revocable letter of credit	Overseas Private Investment Corporation
Irrevocable letter of credit	(OPIC)
Repatriation	International Court of Justice (ICJ)
Payment clause	Arbitration
Choice of language clause	Doctrine of sovereign immunity
Force majeure	Doctrine of act of state

FILL-INS

1._____   This Act is a comprehensive scheme that regulates the export of sensitive goods, technologies, and technical data from the U.S.

2._____   An extremely popular vehicle for establishing a foreign market presence. It is a form of licensing whereby the supplier grants the foreign dealer the right to sell products or services in exchange for a fee.

3._____   It is a written list of six-digit codes to classify goods for customs officials worldwide.

4._____   Refers to the ability of a foreign business or individual to return money earned in the foreign country to its home country.

5._____   This authorizes a business to export nonsensitive goods and is issued by the Office of Export Administration of the Department of Commerce usually without a formal application process.

6._____   This is an important requirement for any international contract and specifies the method and manner in which payment is to be made.

7._____   Operating in this fashion, an international business can undertake manufacturing while maintaining complete ownership of the facilities.

8._____   The primary purposes of this organization are to promote uniformity among tariff schedules affecting international trade and to encourage elimination of legal obstacles encumbering international trade.

9._____   During the Middle Ages, international principles in this governed commercial transactions throughout Europe.

10._____   The Act creates a limited exemption from antitrust laws for businesses that form export trading companies.

11._____   Involves the use of an exporter who sells the product in foreign markets for the U.S. manufacturer.

12._____   Although created principally as a peacekeeping body, it has enjoyed greater success in its economic and social efforts.

13._____   Operating in this manner allows a company to undertake its foreign manufacturing in cooperation with a group of local owners or another foreign group.

14._____   This rate, which will vary depending upon the relative attractiveness of another country's products and the demands of a country's citizens to buy the products of another, causes financial risk in international contracts.

15._____   Is an agreement or assurance by a bank of the buyer to pay a specified amount to the seller upon receipt of documentation proving that the goods have been shipped and that any contractual obligations of the seller have been fulfilled.

16._____   This was created to reduce protectionist barriers, such as subsidies and tariffs, that inhibit international trade.

17._____   Among its basic purposes are the facilitation of the expansion and balanced growth of international trade by stabilizing foreign exchange rates.

18._____   Its purpose is to promote private foreign investment by means of guarantees or participation in loans and other investments made by private investors.

19._____   This agreement involves a contractual arrangement whereby one business grants another business access to its patents and other technologies.

20._____   This is the principal Court of the United Nations, but only countries, not private parties, have standing.

MULTIPLE CHOICE QUESTIONS

Select the best answer to each of the following questions.

1._____   Which of the following is <u>not</u> usually part of the documentation required to collect on a letter of credit?

    a.   Bill of lading.

    b.   Contract between buyer and seller.

    c.   Certificate of origin.

    d.   Export license.

2._____   Which of the following is <u>not</u> one of the groups involved in standardizing arbitration rules and procedures?

    a.   World Court.

    b.   International Chamber of Commerce.

    c.   London Court of Arbitration.

    d.   United Nations Commission on International Law.

    e.   All of the above are involved.

3._____   Which is **not** one of the reasons why the Antidumping Duty Act was created?

    a.   To retaliate against unfair foreign trade practices.

    b.   To assist domestic industries and workers.

    c.   To reduce the advantages of lower costs of production from foreign subsidies.

    d.   To form a free trade zone in North America.

4._____   What is **not** one of the advantages of a joint venture?

    a.   It allows a business to undertake foreign manufacturing by cooperating with local owners or another foreign group.

    b.   It allows virtually any division of ownership.

    c.   It creates a greater degree of managerial control than wholly-owned operations.

    d.   It requires less investment than a wholly-owned operation.

5._____   Which of the following is one of the basic purposes of the International Trade Commission?

    a.   To recommend trade adjustments to the President.

    b.   To facilitate expansion and balanced growth of international trade.

    c.   To aid in elimination of foreign exchange restrictions.

    d.   To shorten duration and lessen disequilibrium in international balance of payments of its members.

6._____   In 700 B.C. a code of international law had been developed in

    a.   Europe and was called the lex mercatoria.

    b.   Egypt.

    c.   England.

    d.   Island of Rhodes.

7._____   A letter of credit:

    a.   Must be irrevocable.

    b.   Is generally issued by a seller of goods.

    c.   Is generally issued by the buyer's bank.

    d.   Is seldom used in international trade.

8._____   The International Court of Justice:

    a.   Is the principal organ of the European Common Market.

    b.   Is headquartered in Geneva.

    c.   Makes decisions involving monetary judgments which may be referred to the United Nations for enforcement.

    d.   Hears cases from citizens of member countries.

9._____   The term "repatriation":

    a.   Refers to the ability of a foreign business to return money earned in a foreign country to its home country.

    b.   Is of slight consequence in international business.

    c.   Is regulated by the United Nations.

    d.   Refers to a uniform method of determining the exchange rate between monies of industrialized nations.

10._____   A positive trade balance

       a.   Is currently enjoyed by the United States.

       b.   Is seldom a desirable state since having a negative trade balance tends to stabilize an economy.

       c.   Means that the value of a country's exports exceeds the value of its imports.

       d.   Means that the value of a country's imports exceeds the value of its exports.

===

MATCHING

a.   Direct exporting

b.   Moller-Butcher v. U.S. Department of Commerce

c.   Contract manufacturing

d.   Choice of law clause

e.   Repatriation

f.   Choice of language clause

g.   Force majeure clause

h.   North American Free Trade Agreement

i.   Empresa Nacional Siderurgica v. U.S.

j.   Nationalization

k.   Tariff

l.   Positive trade balance

m.   Foreign exchange rate reporting market

n.   Foreign Corrupt Practices Act

o.   Specific tariffs

p.   Expropriation

q.   Overseas Private Investment Corporation

r.   World Bank

s.   Franchises

t.   Lex mercatoria

u.   Harper-Wyman Co. v. In-Bond and Hase

v.   Standard Brands Paint Co. Inc. v. U. S.

1._____   It insures investors willing to invest in less-developed countries friendly to the U.S. and in need of social and economic development programs.

2._____   Is defined as the actions of a country in taking foreign assets or other property rights in accordance with international law.

3._____   Is a duty or tax levied by a government on an imported good.

4._____   This occurs when a country makes a decision to take over a foreign investment and is usually related to public or national welfare.

5._____   This case applied the U.S. Antidumping Act to a Spanish steel company.

6._____   The ability of a foreign business or individual to return money earned in the foreign country to its home country. The usual reasons for restricting a businesses ability to take local currencies out of a foreign country are the concern for a reserve shortage in local currencies and the desire that money earned within the country be placed back into the local economy.

7._____   Specifies the law to be applied to any dispute arising among the parties to an international contract.

8._____   This method of doing business with foreign countries involves contracting for the production of products in foreign countries and having the products shipped to the U.S. for sale in retail outlets.

9._____   The most visible of these are fast-food restaurants, hotels, car rentals, soft drinks, and business services.

10._____   Law merchant.

11._____   This clause protects the contracting parties from problems or contingencies beyond their control and is traditionally used to protect parties from the repercussions of a natural disaster that interfered with performance.

12._____   This case upheld the sanctions of the Export Administration Act for reexport violations.

13._____   This imposes a fixed tax or duty on each unit of the product.

14._____   This act prohibits U.S. citizens from bribing foreign officials.

15._____   Initially involves the development of an organization within a business responsible for export business. Goods manufactured here are shipped to foreign customers.

16._____   This is a worldwide system that aids in international transactions by the reporting of values of foreign currencies.

17._____   This sets out the official language by which a contract is to be interpreted.

18._____   It's purpose is to eliminate restrictions on the free flow of goods and capital among the U.S., Canada, and Mexico.

19._____   Is the functional name given to the International Bank for Reconstruction and Development.

20._____   Situation where the value of a country's exports exceeds the value of its imports.

21._____   Held that imported goods, even if unassembled, may be taxed as "entireties" if they are to be assembled later.

22._____   Upheld the choice-of-law agreement in the contract between foreign business partners.

CASE PROBLEMS

1. As the nations of Eastern Europe emerge from the former socialist economies, it is obvious that much financial assistance will be necessary to rebuild them into productive markets. What international organizations may be able to help them, and why?

_____

_____

_____

2. As a new exporter, Paul's Plumbing Company needs to know what government permission will be necessary in order to sell its plastic pipes and connectors to Mexico. Are any tariffs or licenses required?

_____

_____

_____

3. Sally's Shoe Emporium has learned that Guido's Fine Leather Goods has an excellent buy on women's low heeled pumps, which would sell well in the U.S. There are problems about buying them in Italy and importing them to the U.S. However, the leather goods could be imported without the trim and assembled in the U.S., at a considerable savings, if there were a way to do this. What does Sally's need to know about tariffs and assembly areas?

_____

_____

_____

4.   In reference to Sally's proposed transaction, what are three terms of the contract for the purchase of the goods that should be considered as very important in negotiating the deal?

_____

_____

_____

5.   Again in reference to Sally's purchase, should some term be included in the contract that would provide for dispute resolution? If so, what might you suggest?

_____

_____

_____

APPLICATION QUESTIONS

DO YOU AGREE OR DISAGREE WITH THE FOLLOWING STATEMENTS? JOT DOWN YOUR REASONS.

1.   International business is not of concern to Boyd's Barbeque Stand, because it buys all its pork locally and sells only to a local clientele.

       Agree _____   Disagree _____

       Reasons:

2.   If the U.S. became involved in a dispute with Canada over poultry, it must submit the dispute to the WTO for resolution.

       Agree _____   Disagree _____

       Reasons:

3.   If Irmo Importer, a U. S. business, wishes to import computers into the U.S., it makes no difference for tariff purposes whether he imports only the component parts or brings the assembled computer.

Agree _____   Disagree _____

Reasons:

4.   While the Sherman Antitrust Act prohibits trusts that tend to monopolize or restrain trade and commerce, U.S. companies may be exempt from that ban when they participate in exporting activities, because Congress doesn't care whether U.S. firms have unfair trade advantages in foreign markets.

Agree _____   Disagree _____

Reasons:

5.   If Brenda Starr Dress Company wishes to export its products to Belgium, it must apply for a license from the Department of Commerce, because all exports, whether sensitive or nonsensitive, must be cleared by the Office of Export Administration.

Agree _____   Disagree _____

Reasons:

Answer Section

CHAPTER 1

Fill-Ins

1. Common law.
2. Curia Regis.
3. Constitution.
4. Precedent.
5. Administrative agencies.
6. Executive order.
7. Criminal law.
8. Stare Decisis.
9. Beyond a reasonable doubt.
10. Chad.
11. Milton Friedman.
12. Morals.
13. Martin Luther King.
14. Dr. John Ladd.
15. Dr. Melvin Anshen.
16. Ethics.
17. Kenneth Goodpaster.
18. Social contract.
19. Adam Smith.
20. Corporate culture.

Multiple Choice Questions

1.	e		6.	d
2.	d		7.	a
3.	a		8.	a
4.	a		9.	d
5.	c		10.	b

Matching

1.	d		11.	s
2.	h		12.	l
3.	g		13.	p
4.	e		14.	r
5.	c		15.	k
6.	j		16.	q
7.	b		17.	m
8.	a		18.	o
9.	i		19.	n
10.	f		20.	t

Case Problems

1. No, because law is a powerful tool of social change.

2. Yes, although they should try to be impartial.

3. Yes, both by raising the cost of doing business, and sometimes by direct price controls.

4. Yes, because free markets depend on stability and predictability to flourish.

5. Certainly Harry has a legal obligation, and may or may not feel that he has a moral obligation as well.

CHAPTER 2

Fill-Ins

1. Federal Rules of Civil Procedure.
2. Venue.
3. Quasi in rem.
4. Personal service.
5. Long-arm statutes.
6. Congress.
7. Writ of Certiorari.
8. Court of Appeals, Federal Circuit.
9. Jurisdiction.
10. Subject matter jurisdiction.
11. Exclusive jurisdiction.
12. Trial courts.
13. Courts of appeal.
14. Small Claims Courts.
15. Trial de novo.
16. Federal District Courts.
17. Diversity of citizenship.
18. Concurrent jurisdiction.
19. Article III of the U.S. Constitution.
20. Default judgment.

Multiple Choice Questions

1.	a		7.	d
2.	d		8.	c
3.	b		9.	a
4.	d		10.	c
5.	d		11.	e
6.	b		12.	c

Matching

1.	t	11.	l
2.	c	12.	m
3.	d	13.	n
4.	e	14.	i
5.	a	15.	o
6.	b	16.	h
7.	f	17.	p
8.	g	18.	r
9.	j	19.	s
10.	k	20.	q

Case Problems

1. She can recover actual damages for emotional distress caused by the untrue accusations of the National Inquirer and, in addition, punitive damages.

2. Michelle Marvin sued Lee Marvin for breach of contract. The court said she could recover damages if she could prove that a contract existed. She couldn't. This is a state matter.

3. The law of Oklahoma, the state where the accident occurred would normally be used. If for policy reasons the court determined that it was contrary to the policy of the state, the Texas court might apply its own law.

4. The judgment was not valid. The service was not adequate to satisfy the requirements of due process.

5. A California court would have jurisdiction if the corporation had enough ties with California to satisfy the due process requirements of the 14th Amendment.

6. The injury occurred in Georgia, but Alabama may have the most significant interest and therefore be the most convenient forum under Beatty.

CHAPTER 3

Fill-Ins

1.   Opening statements.
2.   General Verdict.
3.   Complaint.
4.   Hung jury.
5.   Demurrer or motion to dismiss for failure to state a cause of action.
6.   Unduly burdensome test.
7.   Written interrogatories.
8.   Answer.
9.   Preponderance of the evidence.
10.   Adversary system of justice.
11.   Reply.
12.   Order for the Production of Documents.
13.   Summary judgment.
14.   Affirmative defense.
15.   Writ of execution.
16.   Voir Dire.
17.   Pretrial conference.
18.   Deposition.
19.   Errors of law.
20.   Closing arguments.

Multiple Choice Questions

1.	e		6.	b
2.	b		7.	d
3.	c		8.	a
4.	d		9.	a
5.	d		10.	e

Matching

1.	p	12.	i
2.	f	13.	a
3.	o	14.	d
4.	e	15.	m
5.	h	16.	r
6.	1	17.	n
7.	k	18.	q
8.	c	19.	g
9.	b	20.	t
10.	j	21.	u
11.	s	22.	v

Case Problems

1. Spillman should take a deposition of Goodman and ask him about the issues she is concerned with. This will preserve and freeze his testimony. She will probably be able to use the deposition if Goodman is unable to testify at trial.

2. He could make a request for admissions. If there are no factual disputes, he can move for a summary judgment.

3. Appeal and argue that the award was excessive.

4. Boyington can use discovery to get information from witnesses through dispositions and interrogations and may request the Court to order production of documents.

5. Flour Mill can ask the court for a writ of execution to enforce the judgment.

CHAPTER 4

Fill-Ins

1. Negotiation.
2. Arbitration.
3. Award.
4. Submission.
5. UNCITRAL.
6. Federal Arbitration Act.
7. Court-annexed arbitration.
8. Compulsory arbitration.

9. United Nations Convention on the Recognition and Enforcement of Foreign Arbitral Awards
10. Negotiation.
11. Mediation.
12. Final offer.
13. Mediator.
14. Society of Professionals in Dispute Resolution.
15. Mini-trial.
16. Summary jury trial.
17. Confidentiality.
18. The Judicial Improvements Act of 1990.
19. The Administrative Dispute Resolution Act of 1990
20. Colorado

Multiple Choice Questions

1. c
2. b
3. e
4. e
5. b
6. e
7. e
8. e
9. d
10. b

Matching

1. j
2. o
3. t
4. s
5. l
6. a
7. p
8. r
9. d
10. m
11. g
12. b
13. q
14. k
15. h
16. n
17. e
18. c
19. f
20. i

Case Problems

1. Thom's has much more control in negotiation and spends much less money and time in bargaining toward a settlement rather than going to litigation. It may also preserve a better relation with the Cooperative by negotiating rather than bringing suit.

2. Yes. The court will enforce the contract.

3.   Yes. It can negotiate with the Cooperative, and can ask for assistance from private groups like the American Arbitration Association.

4.   Probably not, unless the arbitrator has committed grievous error.

5.   Yes, courts will listen to claims for enforcement of awards.

CHAPTER 5

Fill-Ins

1.   Federal Preemption.
2.   Fifth Amendment.
3.   Sixth Amendment.
4.   Due process clause.
5.   Compensation.
6.   Necessary and proper clause.
7.   Warrantless searches of business.
8.   States.
9.   Congress.
10.   Unreasonable search and seizure clause.
11.   Asahi Metal Industry v. Superior Court of California.
12.   Preemptory challenge.
13.   Political speech.
14.   Shapiro v. Kentucky Bar Assn.
15.   Intrastate commerce.
16.   14th Amendment.
17.   Individuals.
18.   Commerce clause.
19.   Federal regulation.
20.   Seventh Amendment.

Multiple Choice Questions

1.	c	6.	c
2.	d	7.	b
3.	d	8.	a
4.	a	9.	c
5.	d	10.	d

Matching

1.	j		11.	k
2.	f		12.	e
3.	d		13.	l
4.	i		14.	g
5.	n		15.	o
6.	q		16.	t
7.	h		17.	s
8.	r		18.	b
9.	a		19.	c
10.	p		20.	m
			21.	u

Case Problems

1. Yes. The statute will be struck down as an impermissible interference with interstate commerce.

2. Yes. They have a right of due process of law, which includes a right to be heard.

3. Yes. This is an impermissible interference with the First Amendment's freedom of the press, and the Fifteenth Amendment's equal protection guarantee.

4. It depends. <u>Central Hudson</u> allowed suppression of promotional advertising by an electric utility company which was less than a total ban, as is this. However, electronic poker is a form of gambling, a business in which there is a substantial governmental interest in protecting the public. If public disorder is caused by the business, the government may have a right to regulate.

5. Probably not, unless notice of these random, warrantless searches was made part of all employees' hiring information. Still these searches may be illegal because they are not related to specific situations involving safety violations or accidents.

CHAPTER 6

Fill-Ins

1. Adjudicatory hearing.
2. Enforcement power.
3. Monitor their own behavior.
4. Administrative agency.
5. Sunset law.

6.   Enabling statute.
7.   Standing.
8.   Administrative law.
9.   Mandatory cost-benefit analysis.
10.   Administrative agencies.
11.   Freedom of Information Act.
12.   Environmental Protection Act.
13.   Rulemaking.
14.   Procedural rules.
15.   Interpretative rules.
16.   Administrative Procedures Act.
17.   Legislative delegation.
18.   Privacy Act.
19.   OSHA.
20.   Substantive rules.

Multiple Choice Questions

1.	d		6.	d
2.	b		7.	c
3.	d		8.	b
4.	c		9.	c
5.	d		10.	c

Matching

1.	k		11.	o
2.	j		12.	a
3.	f		13.	t
4.	e		14.	g
5.	m		15.	h
6.	s		16.	p
7.	1		17.	i
8.	r		18.	d
9.	n		19.	c
10.	q		20.	b

Case Problems

1.   The court should rule for the Secretary of Commerce. The safety measure included children's cribs because it found that people who smoke were frequently around cribs and posed a danger to babies who were unable to protect themselves.

2.   A reviewing court should not overturn the FTC's action. As long as there was evidence to support the agency's actions, the court will not review and reweigh the evidence. A court can only overturn an agency's actions when it has acted in an arbitrary and capricious manner.

3.   The Supreme Court would probably rule that Congress, and not a court, is responsible for the APA and if it is determined that its procedures are not adequate, it will be up to Congress to change it. The rule has been applied effectively many thousands of times.

4.   He can appoint his own people to run the Agency, who will remove or reinterpret old rules in his favor, ask Congress to cut the Agency's budget, and veto any congressional legislation that would strengthen the Agency.

CHAPTER 7

Fill-Ins

1.   False imprisonment.
2.   Private nuisance.
3.   Defamation per se.
4.   Danger invites rescue.
5.   The reasonable person test.
6.   Substantial factor.
7.   Strict liability.
8.   Battery.
9.   Infliction of mental distress.
10.   Trespass.
11.   Tort.
12.   Defamation.
13.   Invasion of privacy.
14.   Intent.
15.   Actual malice.
16.   Truth.
17.   Assault.
18.   Comparative negligence.
19.   Public nuisance.
20.   Trespass to personal property.

Multiple Choice Questions

1.	d		6.	d
2.	a		7.	c
3.	c		8.	d
4.	b		9.	c
5.	b		10.	a

Matching

1.	c		11.	d
2.	t		12.	s
3.	i		13.	n
4.	b		14.	j
5.	h		15.	r
6.	1		16.	f
7.	p		17.	e
8.	o		18.	g
9.	q		19.	k
10.	m		20.	a

Case Problems

1. Yes. Fumigation is ultrahazardous work and cannot be made safe, so those who choose to sell the services can be held strictly liable for harm caused by the chemicals.

2. The court held that Dalton could not recover because his negligence caused the injuries.

3. They should sue in negligence for malpractice, and must show that Bernie failed to meet the reasonable standard of care for accountancy.

4. The right to seek recovery in tort with punitive damages is enjoyed by businesses as well as private individuals.

5. Yes. If they can show that the first barge was negligently secured to its pier and that it was a significant factor in causing their damage. This is a "proximate cause" defense case, similar to the Long Island Railroad's defense.

CHAPTER 8

Fill-Ins

1. Disparagement.
2. Privity of contract.
3. Failure to warn.
4. Caveat emptor.
5. Reasonable care.
6. Interference with contractual relations.
7. Negligence.
8. Strict liability.
9. American Law Institute.
10. Warranty theory.
11. Implied warranty.
12. Premises liability.
13. Implied warranty of safety.
14. Market-share liability.
15. Defenses in product-related injury cases.
16. Warranty of merchantability.
17. Express warranty.
18. Sophisticated purchaser.
19. Failure to warn.
20. Assumption of Risk.

Multiple Choice Questions

1.	b	6.	d
2.	c	7.	a
3.	c	8.	a
4.	d	9.	c
5.	d	10.	c

Matching

1.	a		11.	i
2.	d		12.	k
3.	q		13.	l
4.	g		14.	n
5.	e		15.	p
6.	h		16.	b
7.	c		17.	f
8.	m		18.	t
9.	r		19.	j
10.	s		20.	o

Case Problems

1. She must show negligence in design and failure to warn of a defect which is ultrahazardous.

2. They are both liable under strict liability and negligence for failure to replace the defective filter, failure to warn, and for placing an ultrahazardous product on the market.

3. Yes. It appears that Holly properly prepared the pork. Store is strictly liable.

4. Better to hold the manufacturer liable who could have prevented the defect than to force the injured consumer to bear the cost of the harm; then pass the extra expenses on to the consuming public.

5. The court held for the manufacturer, finding that the danger was obvious and that it was unreasonable to expect it to take precautions against a baby using the product.

CHAPTER 9

Fill-Ins

1. Chattel.
2. Property.
3. Title.
4. Fee simple.
5. Easement.
6. Covenant.
7. Profit.
8. Adverse possession.
9. Tenant.

10. Eminent domain.
11. Police powers.
12. Zoning.
13. Intellectual property.
14. Trademark.
15. Trade dress.
16. Trade name.
17. Fair use.
18. Patent.
19. Trade secret.
20. Infringement.

Multiple Choice Questions

1.	e		6.	a
2.	d		7.	e
3.	a		8.	e
4.	e		9.	a
5.	c		10.	c

Matching

1.	g		11.	c
2.	n		12.	k
3.	p		13.	r
4.	h		14.	t
5.	a		15.	d
6.	i		16.	l
7.	o		17.	s
8.	b		18.	e
9.	j		19.	m
10.	q		20.	f

Case Problems

1. Use a life estate for the handicapped daughter with remainder over to the two other children and their heirs.

2. Put a restrictive covenant of a one story building only on the beach front lot, so as not to block the ocean view for the back lot, and set up an easement on it for a walking path to the beach.

3. Ask the court for a lien on the house until Susi pays.

4.   Barney must use no images, symbols, or trade secrets used by the Mouse.

5.   File with the U.S. Patent office first. Then file an application with the Patent Corporation Treaty for WTO protection.

CHAPTER 10

Fill-Ins

1.   Voidable contracts.
2.   Contractual capacity.
3.   Implied contract.
4.   Statute of frauds.
5.   Bilateral contract.
6.   Uniform Commercial Code (UCC).
7.   Freedom of contract.
8.   Covenant not to compete.
9.   Unenforceable contracts.
10.   Parol evidence rule.
11.   Acceptance.
12.   Rescission.
13.   Substantial performance.
14.   Void contract.
15.   Unilateral contract.
16.   Punitive damages.
17.   Illegal contracts.
18.   Express contracts.
19.   Exculpatory agreements.
20.   Restatement of Contracts.

Multiple Choice Questions

1.	b		6.	c
2.	d		7.	d
3.	b		8.	c
4.	b		9.	b
5.	d		10.	a

Matching

1.	i		11.	b
2.	s		12.	f
3.	d		13.	g
4.	h		14.	r
5.	e		15.	c
6.	j		16.	k
7.	t		17.	q
8.	m		18.	a
9.	o		19.	n
10.	p		20.	l

Case Problems

1. The court held that there was a contract, and it allowed the McNultys to collect the reasonable value of their services.

2. The school district will prevail. The offer, by its terms, had expired when Corcoran attempted to accept it. His acceptance was a counteroffer, which the district chose not to accept.

3. This was not an offer. By its terms, the letter was being sent to several interested parties. It is not reasonable to believe that the realtor had offered one parcel to several potential buyers.

4. The court held that the restrictions were unconscionable and refused to enforce them.

5. A common law judge would say that the agreement was unenforceable due to a lack of consideration. A judge more attuned to the UCC, where no consideration is required for modification, would probably hold that the agreement was unenforceable.

CHAPTER 11

Fill-Ins

1. Battle of the forms.
2. Certificate of deposit.
3. U.N. Convention on the International Sales of Goods.
4. Goods.
5. Trade usage.
6. Cure.
7. Contract modification.
8. Output contract.

9.   Good faith.
10.   Sale.
11.   Open terms contract.
12.   Merchant.
13.   Installment contract.
14.   Negotiation.
15.   Gift.
16.   Firm offer.
17.   Note.
18.   Holder in due course.
19.   Express warranty.
20.   Buyer.
21.   Draft.

Multiple Choice Questions

1.	e	6.	c
2.	d	7.	e
3.	e	8.	e
4.	e	9.	e
5.	e	10.	d

Matching

1.	o	11.	a
2.	r	12.	h
3.	n	13.	l
4.	q	14.	d
5.	f	15.	s
6.	m	16.	i
7.	g	17.	e
8.	k	18.	c
9.	p	19.	t
10.	j	20.	b

Case Problems

1.   He has a duty to provide reasonable care and resell if commercially reasonable.

2.   They needed to include warranty terms and disclaimers; sellers' rights and remedies on breach; and buyers' duties of performance. It is not always necessary to include price, payment and delivery terms.

3. If there is a quantity term and if the seller authenticated the writing, the notes may suffice.

4. Probably not, if there was no extraordinary circumstance involved. Southwire may declare a breach and claim actual damages.

5. Annie might call Old Trusty to verify the authenticity of the initial transaction, but if the document is unflawed on the issue of negotiability, and the circumstances are not suspicious, then Annie is probably a HDC.

CHAPTER 12

Fill-Ins

1. Open account.
2. Security.
3. Personal property.
4. Mortgage.
5. Security interest.
6. Perfected.
7. Lien.
8. Equity financing.
9. Suretyship.
10. Subrogation.
11. Floating lien.
12. Statutory redemption period
13. Bankruptcy Reform Act of 1978.
14. Trustee.
15. Priority classes.
16. Chapter 11.
17. Composition.
18. Extension.
19. Assignment.
20. Secured transaction.

Multiple Choice Questions

1.	c		6.	e
2.	d		7.	c
3.	a		8.	e
4.	e		9.	a
5.	e		10.	a

Matching

1.	t		11.	i
2.	a		12.	r
3.	q		13.	l
4.	c		14.	e
5.	m		15.	h
6.	o		16.	n
7.	b		17.	k
8.	s		18.	p
9.	d		19.	j
10.	f		20.	g

Case Problems

1. He can negotiate to purchase on credit from his supplier or obtain a working capital loan or arrange for surety to co-sign for a loan.

2. Not necessarily. Article 9 requires that the debtor sign a security agreement and financing statement before the creditor may attach George's collateral, and requires the creditor to file the financing statement before perfection.

3. No. If George knows the customer's character and capacity to pay to be honorable and sound, he may choose to operate an open account without any security other than the customer's promise to pay.

4. No. He should try to work with his bank and other supplier / creditors to reschedule his debt repayments. Bankruptcy is a last resort.

5. He may choose Chapter 11 to reorganize his business which is often preferable to a Chapter 7 liquidation proceeding. Chapter 13 is only available for personal debts.

CHAPTER 13
Fill-Ins

1. Termination by operation of law.
2. Apparent authority.
3. Actual authority.
4. Duty of reasonable care.
5. Universal agents.
6. Duty to account.
7. Ratification.

8. Independent contractor.
9. Agent.
10. Subagent.
11. Duty to indemnify.
12. Duty to cooperate with the agent.
13. Express ratification.
14. Agency coupled with an interest.
15. Implied authority.
16. Fiduciary relationship.
17. Agency through operation of law.
18. Duty of loyalty.
19. Agency by Estoppel.
20. Agency relationship.

Multiple Choice Questions

1.	a		6.	d
2.	d		7.	b
3.	a		8.	a
4.	b		9.	c
5.	c		10.	c

Matching

1.	p		11.	a
2.	k		12.	d
3.	o		13.	s
4.	i		14.	j
5.	h		15.	l
6.	f		16.	q
7.	g		17.	c
8.	e		18.	n
9.	r		19.	m
10.	t		20.	b

Case Problems

1. Yes. The bank president agreed to serve as an agent for the Alexanders and breached his duty to them by failing to advise them that termites were on the property.

2. No. This is an irrevocable agency coupled with an interest.

3.   Black must be an independent contractor under the ABC test. Black then must pay his own taxes.

4.   The court held LIC liable under the doctrine of <u>respondeat</u> <u>superior</u>. Employers are held liable for the torts of their employees because the employer selects the employee and controls him and should be liable for his negligence.

5.   The seller can sue the agent whom she/he dealt with as well as the undisclosed principals, the Rockefellers.

CHAPTER 14

Fill-Ins

1.   Joint venture.
2.   Syndicate.
3.   Partnership agreement.
4.   General incorporation statutes.
5.   Joint stock company.
6.   Dissolution.
7.   Limited partnerships.
8.   General partnership.
9.   Fiduciary duty of loyalty.
10.   Winding up.
11.   Bylaws.
12.   Cooperative.
13.   Franchise.
14.   Shareholders.
15.   Partners.
16.   FTC Franchise Rule.
17.   Dissolution.
18.   Sole proprietorship.
19.   Business Judgment Rule.
20.   Limited Liability Company.

Multiple Choice Questions

1.	c		6.	d
2.	b		7.	b
3.	b		8.	d
4.	b		9.	d
5.	b		10.	d

Matching

1.	c		11.	t
2.	f		12.	a
3.	g		13.	h
4.	i		14.	k
5.	r		15.	l
6.	p		16.	e
7.	s		17.	q
8.	j		18.	d
9.	o		19.	n
10.	m		20.	b

Case Problems

1.   Yes. Franchises are regulated by the FTC and by states, to protect the rights of franchise owners.

2.   Joint venture.

3.   No. He is not actively participating in the day to day management of the partnership.

4.   Yes. They co-owned a business for profit.

5.   No. They are liable. The business judgment rule is not a defense to pay kickbacks and bribes.

CHAPTER 15

Fill-Ins

1.   NLRA, Section 8(c).
2.   Lock out.
3.   Occupation licensure.
4.   Employee handbook.
5.   Wagner Act (NLRA).
6.   Workers' compensation statutes.
7.   Landrum Griffin Act.
8.   Collective bargaining.
9.   Primary boycott.
10.   Federal Minimum Wage requirements.
11.   Concerted Activities.
12.   Right to work statutes.
13.   National Institute of Occupational Safety and Health (NIOSH).
14.   Employment-at-will.
15.   Unfair labor practices.
16.   Secondary boycott.
17.   Whistle blower.
18.   Drug testing.
19.   Duty of fair bargaining.
20.   Arbitration clauses.

Multiple Choice Questions

1.   b   6.   c
2.   d   7.   b
3.   c   8.   c
4.   d   9.   b
5   d   10.   c

Matching

1.	k		11.	h
2.	f		12.	l
3.	n		13.	t
4.	a		14.	s
5.	e		15.	b
6.	o		16.	r
7.	m		17.	i
8.	g		18.	d
9.	p		19.	j
10.	q		20.	c

Case Problems

1. No. They are obligated to pay agency fees.

2. Send him home with a sober driver, consult the collective progressive discipline, and consider rehabilitation.

3. Yes, if the EPA protects whistle blowers, or if his state's common law protects him against wrongful discharge.

4. She may have whistle blowers' protection against Pete, but Pete has the right to defend and/or justify his actions.

5. His employer, if he was injured in an accident arising out of and in the course of his employment.

CHAPTER 16

Fill-Ins

1. Age Discrimination in Employment Act.
2. Discriminate.
3. Workforce analysis.
4. Pregnancy Discrimination Act.
5. Executive Order.
6. Protected Classes.
7. Constructive Discharge.
8. Handicapped individual.

9.   Underutilization analysis.
10.   Equal Pay Act.
11.   Title VII of Civil Rights Act of 1964.
12.   Affirmative action program.
13.   BFOQ.
14.   Business necessity.
15.   Disparate treatment.
16.   Americans with Disabilities Acts.
17.   Differential Standards Doctrine.
18.   EEOC.
19.   Disparate Impact.
20.   Reverse discrimination.

Multiple Choice Questions

1.	d	6.	d
2.	d	7.	b
3.	c	8.	c
4.	a	9.	a
5.	a	10.	c

Matching

1.	d	11.	i
2.	m	12.	j
3.	1	13.	h
4.	p	14.	k
5.	b	15.	t
6.	q	16.	s
7.	c	17.	r
8.	e	18.	o
9.	f	19.	a
10.	g	20.	n

Case Problems

1.   His best argument is that of discriminatory treatment, while the employer will argue that it had no duty to hire back any former workers.

2.   Their best argument involves discriminatory impact, while the prison system will argue BFOQ.

3.   They will show that they are following an affirmative action plan under EEOC or a court order.

4.   She will argue "hostile environment" under <u>Harris</u> and the employer will argue that she welcomed Evans behavior.

5.   Her age and their potential liability under ADEA.

CHAPTER 17

Fill-Ins

1.   Clean Air Act.
2.   EPA.
3.   Manifest.
4.   Bubble concept.
5.   The Silent Spring.
6.   Private nuisance.
7.   LAER Standards.
8.   Strict liability.
9.   Manifest system.
10.   Pollution.
11.   Trespass.
12.   Montreal Protocol.
13.   Hazardous waste.
14.   BACT Standards.
15.   Public nuisance.
16.   Ozone.
17.   State implementation plans (SIPs)
18.   Superfund.
19.   Acid rain.
20.   Clean Water Act.

Multiple Choice Questions

1.	b		6.	c
2.	e		7.	a
3.	c		8.	b
4.	d		9.	d
5.	d		10.	b

Matching

1.	i		11.	q
2.	t		12.	s
3.	b		13.	r
4.	p		14.	f
5.	c		15.	g
6.	k		16.	h
7.	o		17.	j
8.	a		18.	d
9.	e		19.	n
10.	m		20.	l

Case Problems

1. No, because Congress has already passed a law permitting imposition of penalties.

2. Yes, but not in the determination of the National Ambient Air Quality Standards.

3. The court decided not to close down the plant in part because of the economic repercussions on the community. Some observers, however, argue that those factors should not be considered.

4. No, under the reserved powers of the Constitution.

5. No. TOSCA was intended to identify hazardous substance before they were marketed. EPA has used its ban or restricted existing chemicals.

CHAPTER 18

Fill-Ins

1. The Nutrition Labeling and Education Act of 1990.
2. Deception policy statement.
3. Learned intermediary doctrine.
4. Advertising substantiation doctrine.
5. Kefauver Amendment.
6. Mail Order Rule.
7. Trade Regulation rules.
8. Delaney clause.
9. Consent decrees.
10. Magnuson Moss Warranty Act.
11. Pure Food and Drugs Act of 1906.
12. Regulation B.
13. Disclosure requirement.
14. Fair Credit Reporting Act.
15. Truth in Lending Act.
16. Electronic Funds Transfer Act.
17. Consumer Credit Protection Act.
18. Consumer Leasing Act.
19. The Jungle.
20. Fair Credit Collections Act.
21. Fair Credit Billing Act.

Multiple Choice Questions

1.	b		6.	c
2.	a		7.	a
3.	e		8.	c
4.	d		9.	c
5.	d		10.	d

Matching

1.	e		11.	o
2.	c		12.	n
3.	d		13.	s
4.	b		14.	p
5.	f		15.	l
6.	j		16.	q
7.	g		17.	r
8.	h		18.	k
9.	a		19.	m
10.	i		20.	t

Case Problems

1. Yes, under the <u>Park</u> decision, the FDA may prosecute.

2. If she reports the theft promptly, she will be liable only for the first $50 in charges.

3. He may consult the FTC Insulation R Value Regulations.

4. She should notify Don and request an opportunity to renegotiate the terms of her payment plan. She may also claim a violation of Regulation Z which required disclosure of the annual percentage rate.

5. A prescribed list of nutrients must be listed by standard serving size to help consumers make informed purchases.

CHAPTER 19

Fill-Ins

1. Per se.
2. Integration.
3. Clayton Act.
4. Merger guidelines.
5. Private parties.
6. Geographic market.
7. Federal Trade Commission.
8. Relevant market.
9. Clayton Act.

10.   Horizontal merger.
11.   Rule of reason.
12.   McCarren-Ferguson Act.
13.   Cartel.
14.   Failing firm defense.
15.   Sherman Act.
16.   Horizontal restraints.
17.   Dango system.
18.   Federal Trade Commission Act.
19.   Resale Price Maintenance agreement.
20.   Dr. Miles rule.
21.   Sharp rule.
22.   Robinson Patman Act.
23.   Volume discounts.
24.   Vertical merger.
25.   Price discrimination.
26.   Retailer's cartel.
27.   Boycott.
28.   Cost justification defense.
29.   Market power.
30.   Vertical exclusionary practice.
31.   Tying arrangement.
32.   Meeting competition.
33.   Territorial restrictions.

Multiple Choice Questions

1.	d	11.	a
2.	e	12.	b
3.	b	13.	b
4.	a	14.	a
5.	d	15.	b
6.	a	16.	d
7.	d	17.	b
8.	c	18.	c
9.	d	19.	a
10.	a	20.	e

Matching *(Horizontal Arrangements)*

1.	m		11.	c
2.	n		12.	f
3.	a		13.	i
4.	d		14.	j
5.	e		15.	l
6.	s		16.	r
7.	b		17.	t
8.	q		18.	g
9.	p		19.	h
10.	o		20.	k

Matching *(Vertical Arrangements)*

1.	a		11.	t
2.	n		12.	o
3.	m		13.	g
4.	d		14.	h
5.	l		15.	i
6.	r		16.	k
7.	s		17.	p
8.	q		18.	c
9.	e		19.	f
10.	b		20.	j

Case Problems

1. Probably so, because of the harm to the U.S. market.

2. Probably not. A merger with one of the larger companies, however, might attract attention.

3. They should consult merger guidelines and consider forming one company. Otherwise, they may be found in violation of the antitrust laws.

4. No, under the failing firm defense.

5. Bigness alone is not evidence of antitrust violations.

6. Yes, if "Hungry Herman's" can show a cost justification or need to meet competition.

CHAPTER 20

Fill-Ins

1.   Safe harbor.
2.   _Howey_ test.
3.   Blue sky laws.
4.   Prospectus.
5.   Accredited investors.
6.   10-K.
7.   Regulation D.
8.   Rule 10-b (5).
9.   Shelf registration.
10. Underwriter.
11. No-load fund.
12. Investment company.
13. Investment companies.
14. Insiders.
15. Stock exchanges.
16. Insider Trading Sanctions Act.
17. Arbitration.
18. OTC.
19. Tender offer.
20. National Association of Security Dealers.

Multiple Choice Questions

1.	c		6.	c
2.	c		7.	d
3.	b		8.	d
4.	d		9.	d
5.	c		10.	a

Matching

1.	e		11.	r
2.	b		12.	s
3.	a		13.	t
4.	f		14	k
5.	c		15.	l
6.	d		16.	g
7.	o		17.	q
8.	i		18.	m
9.	h		19.	p
10.	j		20.	n

Case Problems

1. The common law of agency for violation of fiduciary duties, misrepresentation and fraud, and Section 10b of the 1934 Securities Act.

2. Yes, a nonpurchaser can sue.

3. Yes, because of his abuse of insider knowledge.

4. Yes, because of Billy's scalping violation, they may use the Investment Advisor's Act and seek arbitration.

5. The statute is upheld. It has no effect on the Commerce Clause and does protect the state's citizens.

CHAPTER 21

Fill-Ins

1. Export Administration Act.
2. Franchising.
3. Harmonized tariff schedule
4. Repatriation.
5. General license.
6. Payment clause.
7. Wholly-owned subsidiary.
8. WTO.
9. Lex mercatoria.

10. Export Trading Company Act.
11. Indirect exporting.
12. United Nations.
13. Joint venture.
14. Foreign exchange rate.
15. Letter of credit.
16. General Agreement on Tariffs and Trade (GATT).
17. International Monetary Fund.
18. World Bank.
19. Licensing agreement.
20. International Court of Justice.

Multiple Choice Questions

1.	b		6.	d
2.	a		7.	c
3.	d		8.	c
4.	c		9.	a
5.	a		10.	c

Matching

1.	q		12.	b
2.	p		13.	o
3.	k		14.	n
4.	j		15.	a
5	i		16.	m
6	e		17.	f
7.	d		18.	h
8.	c		19.	r
9.	s		20.	l
10.	t		21.	v
11.	g		22.	u

Case Problems

1. The World Bank may lend money to private investors, while the IMF may lend money to member countries.

2. Yes. He must apply to the Department of Commerce for a general license.

3. She need to become familiar with the harmonized tariff schedules, the issue of "entireties," and free trade zones.

4. She should include a payment clause for currency exchange rate problems, a choice of law clause, and a choice of language clause.

5. Yes. She should investigate the services provided by the American Arbitration Association or the London Court of Arbitration, for example, and include such a provision.